DHARMAKĪRTI'S HETUBINDU

CRITICALLY EDITED BY

ERNST STEINKELLNER

CHINA TIBETOLOGY RESEARCH CENTER

AUSTRIAN ACADEMY OF SCIENCES

Sanskrit Texts from the Tibetan Autonomous Region

founded by

Lhagpa Phuntshogs and **Ernst Steinkellner**

edited in chief by

Dramdul, Ernst Steinkellner, Harunaga Isaacson

No.19

中国藏学研究中心

奥地利科学院

西藏自治区梵文文本系列丛书

创办人

拉巴平措 与 恩斯特·斯坦因凯勒

主编

郑堆，恩斯特·斯坦因凯勒，春永·艾萨克森

第十九卷

CHINA TIBETOLOGY RESEARCH CENTER

AUSTRIAN ACADEMY OF SCIENCES

Dharmakīrti's Hetubindu

Critically edited by

Ernst Steinkellner

on the basis of preparatory work by

Helmut Krasser †

with a transliteration of the Gilgit fragment by

Klaus Wille

CHINA TIBETOLOGY PUBLISHING HOUSE

AUSTRIAN ACADEMY OF SCIENCES PRESS

BEIJING – VIENNA 2016

Angenommen durch die philosophisch–historische Klasse der Österreichischen Akademie der Wissenschaften

ISBN 978-3-7001-7960-7

Printed by Peking Longchang Weiye Print Ltd.

DEDICATED IN GRATITUDE

TO LUDO ROCHER

ON HIS 90th BIRTHDAY

Contents

Acknowledgments

Because of the sad circumstance in producing the editions of the *Hetubindu* manuscript, a word of acknowledgment and on responsibilities is due before introducing the editions proper.

When we had received a copy of the almost complete *codex unicus* of the *Hetubindu*, I thought it appropriate to entrust Helmut Krasser with the work of editing instead of taking it up myself. I passed on to Krasser, therefore, all my notes and corrections to the editions of 1967 as well as on further testimonies collected over the years since then, and in August 2004 he began to work on this manuscript. By October 2004 he had finished the transliteration, made a first correction from October 7 to December 12, 2004, and in 2005 began to work on the critical edition[1] which he then converted to Devanāgarī script. In the summer term of 2012 he presented to his students at Vienna University an already established text for §§ b.12211–b.1221531 and d.2221 of the *Hetubindu*.

By the spring of 2012 Krasser told me that both his diplomatic and critical editions were finished. He did not show them to anyone, however, except for the diplomatic edition to Dania Huber and sections of the critical edition to Hideyo Ogawa and Parimal Patil. Right after the *apoha*-workshop at our institute (April 16–20, 2012) his illness became evident and was soon diagnosed as serious. This work receded into the background of our mind; for we, deeply concerned, slowly realized that all we could do was help him in his last heroic fight. When Helmut Krasser passed away on March 30, 2014, we had to think about how to continue the various projects he had been responsible for until then. My colleagues at the institute who had worked with Krasser in teams decided that Horst Lasic should take the responsibility for the work on the *Madhyamakāvatārabhāṣya* chapters 1 to 5 and on

[1] The first file is dated September 10, 2005, the last December 6, 2008.

the *Pramāṇasamuccayaṭīkā* chapter 5 with a new team, and I was asked to take care of the *Hetubindu*.

Luckily, the diplomatic and critical editions, already composed in Devanāgarī script with the Critical Text Editor program (CTE), were safely kept on the institute's server. Krasser's own computer was inaccessible until July 2014. I first had a look at the diplomatic transliteration and corrected it (June 3–16, 2014). When Krasser's personal files became accessible, I found that the diplomatic edition had already been corrected once by Dania Huber (July 7, 2013). This is gratefully acknowledged. I compared her notes and could add some to my own. Another file contained the most valuable collection of parallel texts found by Koji Ezaki in Śākyabuddhi's *Pramāṇavārttikaṭīkā* and sent to Krasser on August 4, 2010.[2] Moreover, Klaus Wille had informed Krasser of the Gilgit fragment and sent him a transliteration (July 26, 2001). After I contacted Wille, he sent me a photo and several detailed ones of this fragment, and conceded to having this fragment incorporated into the present edition. I am most grateful to Klaus Wille for being able to include this minute treasure so particularly valuable for its age and the utmost proximity to Dharmakīrti's lifetime.

Although Krasser certainly would have further improved upon his critical edition, his final text was not yet developed to a state that would have allowed me to edit it with only minor changes as Krasser's own edition of the text which I had originally hoped. In fact, it turned out that I had to take full responsibility for both editions "on the basis of preparatory work by Helmut Krasser." Saving the time for inputting both texts again and converting the critical text to Devanāgarī was the major advantage of this heritage. Not being an expert user of the CTE program I worked on a pdf file prepared by Horst Lasic from Krasser's CTE text. All changes and additions were then incorporated into the CTE

[2] Ezaki discovered the long *Hetubindu* excerpt in PVṬ$_t$ 168b4–173b3 which exactly parallels HB 10,13–25,6.

file by Heidrun Jäger. She subsequently also added the CTE file of the diplomatic edition, Wille's transliteration of the Srinagar fragment, as well as the introduction, analytic survey and bibliography, thus producing the final layout of the book. My sincere gratitude is due to Heidrun Jäger for her most careful work and for many improvements in regard to sandhi and word separation, as well as to Cristina Pecchia who thoroughly read the final product and made valuable suggestions, and to Luo Hong for spotting a number of typos. Last but not least, I would like to thank Shōryū Katsura and Birgit Kellner for earlier indications of several misprints and misunderstandings in the texts, the translation and the notes of 1967 as fruits of their reading.

Vienna, May 2015 Ernst Steinkellner

Introduction

Various pieces of information still valid can be found in the introduction to HB_{St}, such as on the *Hetubindu* and its historical and literary position, the commentaries on it, and on the Tibetan translation. In the meantime a third commentary was found among the treasures still kept in the Tibetan Autonomous Region: an extensive *Hetubinduṭīkāvyākhyā* by a Nepalese *mahāmaṇḍalācāryapaṇḍitarāja* named Śubha(?)-yabhadra (the manuscript is indistinct) in the colophon. The manuscript is in two possibly 11th century scripts.[3] This is a hitherto unknown work of 123 folios which was seemingly unknown to the later Indian tradition and never translated into Tibetan. A copy of this work is held by the library of the CTRC (box 179).[4]

The Tibetan translation of the *Hetubindu* by Prajñāvarman and dPal brtsegs, probably elaborated already before 800 CE, has been edited in HB_{St}. This edition is referred to in the critical apparatus.

In the introduction to HB_{St} (p. 27), I characterized as novelties in the *Hetubindu* the central position of the purely logical topic, the theory of the logical reason and the elaboration of the formal structures of the theory of reason and of inference, with precise and polished formulations which often take on the character of veritable terminological formulas, such as *sādhyaviparyaye bādhakapramāṇam* (HB 5, 5–6). This is true, of course, but it is not all. And in terms of content the logical theory as such is not new either. What is truly new to a great extent in the *Hetubindu* is found in the three extensive digressions of §§ b, c, and d.

---

[3] I gratefully acknowledge the help received from Alexander von Rospatt and Kashinath Tamot in deciphering this colophon difficult to read.

[4] It is this work that has already been mentioned by Leonard van der Kuijp (Kuijp 2013: note 3).

In digression d, Dharmakīrti deals with his teacher Īśvarasena's theorem of the reason with six characteristics (*ṣaḍlakṣaṇo hetu*). In refuting the three characteristics proposed in addition to Dignāga's three, Dharmakīrti argues once more in support of his own theorem of the three types of reason (*trividhā hetu*) as the only option for satisfying Dignāga's theorem. I assume that with a view to his closer intellectual and social milieu a discussion of his teacher's theorem was deemed unavoidable when rounding up his own new logic. Because he felt obliged to address this topic, Dharmakīrti provides us with otherwise unknown detailed knowledge of this theorem, which remains a historically interesting step in the development of Buddhist logic.

The other digressions b and c, however, go far beyond logical theory proper. Digression c first considers the very nature of non-perception, an epistemological examination, and then examines in detail in what sense this type of cognition can serve as a logical reason.

Digression b serves to underpin his concept of essence^C as reason by elaborating on the cognition of the logical nexus in the case of the proof of the momentariness of all entities.[5] In this digression the nexus is at length established by arguing against the possibility of the cessation of entities under the influence of other causes than their own. Here he uses arguments from previous stages of his proof from cessation (*vināśitvānumāna*), while it is only in conclusion that he draws shortly upon the proof from beingness (*sattvānumāna*) as developed in the *Pramāṇaviniścaya*.[6] In other words, the main part of this digression is devoted to an examination of causality or the function of causes.

---

[5] The historical importance of this digression was already recognized in Yoshimizu 2003: 197–198.

[6] It is noteworthy, however, that already the example he gives in § 3.31 of the *Hetubindu* – where he explains the ascertainment of common presence (*anvayaniścaya*) in the case of an essence^C as reason – is a complete inference of momentariness from beingness (*sattvānumāna*).

My German translation of 1967 followed the reconstruction of the Sanskrit text which is conditioned, aside from the numerous secondary witnesses, by the Tibetan translation and its syntax. At times this amounts to a school-boyish and somewhat pedantic style that often poorly compares with Dharmakīrti's original words now available.[7] Dharmakīrti's manner of using the potentials of Sanskrit syntax for emphases, ellipses and implications with perfect clarity and stylistic beauty is hardly surpassed. As a translation of the *Hetubindu* that we now have before us, the 1967 translation would be in need of improvement in many places. Nevertheless, the meaning of Dharmakīrti's sentences is, in general, not too badly accounted for. Most of the notes are still useful for understanding the argument and the context from and against which he composed his work. Of course, the progress of scholarship in the last decades[8] and the new availability of major works by Dharmakīrti and his opponents have out-dated some historical observations, and a few notes now appear to be flatly wrong. In short I would say that the 1967 book is still useful to a judicious reader, and since the translation by P. P. Gokhale (1997) suffers from the same circumstance, a new English translation remains a desideratum.

[7] A comparison of the 1967 reconstruction with the traditional text here presented clearly exemplifies the types of success and failure possible in attempts of regaining lost Sanskrit texts, and may be useful as training ground for students. Cf. the succinct methodological observations in Lasic 2011: 233–235.

[8] Of particular import are the publications of Claus Oetke (1993) and Chizuko Yoshimizu (2003).

The Potala manuscript

Description

A photostat copy of the palm leaf manuscript with 25 folios is held by the library of the China Tibetology Research Center (CTRC), box 112/1. These folios are contained on seven sheets, with four recto and verso pages on each sheet. The last sheet bears three folios of another text, the *Nānavāda-sthānapustaka* (see below). An additional sheet shows the two wooden covers, one with three Bodhisattvas, the other with two Bodhisattvas and Śākyamuni in the centre, offering deities accompanying each of them on both sides.

Except for f. 25 which is broken off on the left side the manuscript is complete. Only a few folios are blotted (ff. 12a, 17b, 21b, 22b). The folios measure 27,6 by 4,7 cm, with a binding hole to the left of the centre within a blank square space of ca. five *akṣara*s from the second to the fourth or fifth line. The pages bear five to six lines (only f. 11a has four lines). The folios are numbered with numerals on the left side of each reverse page.[9]

The original manuscript is kept at the Potala. From which monastic institution it came from, is nowhere indicated and it was also not possible to determine its original home.

---

[9] Luo Zhao gives the following information in his catalogue (Luo Zhao 1985: 90): "The *Hetubindu* (in Tibetan: *gTan tshigs thigs pa*). In total 25 folios, complete, only about one fifth of the text on the last folio is lost. The length of the folios is 27.6 cm, the breadth is 4.7 cm; each side of the folios has 5 to 6 lines of Sanskrit text written in Dhārikā script in ink (there is one side of a folio that has only 4 lines). This treatise is an important *pramāṇa* work, one of the Seven *Pramāṇa* Works. In the colophon, the author is mentioned as Fa Cheng (Dharmakīrti, in Tibetan: Chos grags)." (Translation Luo Hong)

The script

The script is early proto-Bengālī of probably the 13th century CE.[10] A conspicuous feature is the frequent deviation from the usual *pṛṣṭhamātrā* form of the vowels *e*, *o*. These cases are transliterated in the diplomatic edition as *ê*, *ô*. The *ā* written by a small upper line flag-like hook is also indicated as *â*, although typically used only in tight spaces. This hook is also occasionally used for writing *o*. The *e* and *o* are regular in both types, *pṛṣṭhamātrā* and superscript; *i* is mostly superscript, but the form with down stroke in front also occurs.[11]

Occasionally a *t* with integrated *virāma* (transliterated as t')[12] is found in the later part of the manuscript.

Degemination of *t* before *v*, and gemination of *g*, *t*, *n*, *m*, *v* after *r* are regular.

Additions to the text by a correcting hand in the same script are mostly found in the upper and lower margins with line references and corresponding insertion signs. Corrections are rarely found within the lines of the text. Other additions are explanatory marginalia (glosses by a reader) again in the same script but by another hand.

---

[10] Notwithstanding the fact that already a great variety of names are in currency among scholarship of the last century, I am still tempted to propose yet another name for the script used by the scribes in the scriptoria and monasteries (*vihāra*) of the Pāla realm: the name **Vihārī**. Such a designation would unequivocally highlight the spread of this type of script over areas that in later and modern times not only correspond to Bengal but also, and more importantly to Bihar and Nepal, the later scripts of which are all derived from the one used during the centuries of one of the last great periods of Buddhist culture in India.

[11] These shifts from *pṛṣṭhamātrā* to superscript strokes are also displayed in Vibhūticandra's manuscript of Manorathanandin's *Pramāṇavārttikavṛtti* (cf. Pecchia 2015: 104). This manuscript was copied in all probability during Vibhūticandra's first stay in Tibet between 1204 and 1214 (cf. Pecchia 2015: 107).

[12] This is called *khaṇḍa-ta* in the Bengālī (thanks to Prof. Hans Harder, Heidelberg University).

Notable are also faint half, full and double *daṇḍa*s that were seemingly added by a later reader. These are also reported in the diplomatic edition.

From the beginning of folio 24a5 to the end of folio 24b the script displays a clear slant to the left while remaining the same. Since in what remains of folio 25b the manuscript is straight again, a change of scribes can be excluded.

Filling signs: Throughout the major part of the manuscript a space filling sign [illegible] is used. In the later part, two different filling signs occur: [illegible] (20a4, 23b5 twice, 24a1), and [illegible] (23a4, 24a5, 24a6). As usual, small spaces before the end of a line or before the square left for the binding hole are filled by deleted or broken *daṇḍa*s.

The manuscript shows numerous small empty spaces in the size of one or two *akṣara*s. This indicates that the scribe left these open during the act of copying. This was in most cases done, as I explained in the description of ms C of the *Pramāṇaviniścaya*,[13] because he could not read what I assume had been heavily deleted, erased, or blotted in his exemplar.[14] But there also must have been larger spaces left open by the scribe at first. In a second step, and after taking recourse to another manuscript of the text, some of these open spaces were filled with text either by the scribe or a corrector. This is only visible, of course, when the additional *akṣara*s had to be literally squeezed into the available small space. Examples are: °*ṇāt* // o // (4a3), °*tvasya* // (5a2), °*vākyaprayoga* (6a3), *tadava*° (6b5), °*ttulya*° (9a3), *gamanañ ca* (18b2), or with more space left open or available in the binding square, and by another hand: *mahāprabhāvasya bhavato* (10b5) or *prayoga* (6a4). Thus, it is clear that such text considered correct was copied and sometimes had to be squeezed in, while spaces provisionally introduced by the scribe to accommodate for

[13] Cf. PVin 1–2: xxii–xxiii and PVin 3: xxxiii–xxxiv.

[14] Isaacson 2009: 19 points to yet another possible reason: "to cover an area which was deemed less suitable for copying on, because of a minor flaw in the palm-leaf."

unreadable parts of the exemplar were later recognized as correct deletions or erasures when compared to the other manuscript and were then left as they stand, if only small, or were filled by means of the filling signs indicated above. The question I cannot answer in the case of the present manuscript is why not all of these smaller open spaces were filled alike. In some of these cases the quality of the available black-and-white copy does not allow us any final judgement. An explanation of these remaining open spaces has to await the much desired availability of coloured scans of the original manuscript.[15]

Notes on the lines following the end of the *Hetubindu* text, and on three folios contained in the last sheet of the photos

1. The colophon of the *Hetubindu* manuscript (f. 25b1) is followed by two passages, each written by a different hand: the first (f. 25b2–3) in a rough proto-Bengālī script, the second (f. 25b4–7) in a regular and smaller proto-Bengālī script. I cannot trace the text in these lines but, in terms of their content, I consider the second text to be notes by a student. Below is a transliteration — for the first passage highly tentative — of these lines.

(f. 25b2) ///no bāhyaṃ na ca vedanaṃ na ca tadākāro na cāropito bādhādhivyavasāya‹saṃśaya[ṃ]› c/vidyaṃ saṃgacchate gocaraḥ (3) ///[..]t* hrīnavivekino ja[.]v/cidasyā[ro]pyamāṇ{e}ātma[{..}]nā bāhyatvaṃ vi[{.e}]nāne ’rtha[ḥ] / na dhiyā saṃsṛjyate [..]āntyathā //

(f. 25b4) /// /nāśahetoḥ kiṃ ghaṭaḥ ⊙ syāt' / kiṃ vā vināśaḥ / atmana vināśo [bhava]nn api / kiṃ vā bhāvasvabhāvaḥ syād abhāvo vā / bhā[v]o pi bhāva[.]/// (5) ///dṛśyo vā syād adṛśyo ⊙ vā / dṛśyo pi bhavann a[...][gha]ṭāt' kiṃ pṛthak* / apṛthak* vā /

---

15 As strongly demanded in Isaacson 2009 and explained as to its present prospects in Steinkellner 2014: note 6.

yadi pṛthak* syāt' / kathaṃ ghaṭo naśyati / na [.i]/// (6) ///vadatte samutpanne yajñadatto vinaśyati / apṛthak* cet' / na / tanniṣpattāv aniṣpannasya ta[t]svabhāvatayo.. / asvabhāvatvena ghaṭasya kiṃ/// (7) ///syāt' / adṛśyaś cet' / tat sattāsādhakaṃ pramāṇaṃ na syāt' //

2. The last two sheets of the photos include also the first three folios of a collective manuscript the title of which is given on folio 1a as *Nānāvādasthānapustakaṃ*. This manuscript has been described by Luo Zhao as follows: "*A Treatise on the Reliance on Various Arguments* (*Nānāvādasthānasusthakam*), an abbreviated Tibetan title: *rTsod pa'i gnas sna tshogs*. In total 21 folios, incomplete. The length of the folios is 30.5 cm, the breadth 5.6 cm; each side of the folios has 6 to 7 lines of Sanskrit text written in Dhārikā script in ink. This book is a collection of different works by several authors; the contents are philosophical and logical arguments. So far, among the authors, Jñānaśrīmitra and Jitāri have been identified."[16] (Translation Luo Hong)

A copy of this manuscript in the Potala is held in the library of the CTRC (box 112/2, sheets 8 to 14). Together with the three recto pages on the last sheet of the *Hetubindu* manuscript there are in all 21 folios. The text is incomplete. This manuscript contains a number of short texts by Jñānaśrīmitra, Jitāri, and other authors, and will possibly be edited in the future by Luo Hong and myself.

[16] Sandhak, too, in his list (p. 91) gives *Nānāvādasthānasusthakam* as the name. Luo Zhao's reading was recorded in Steinkellner/Much 1995: xx.

The *Hetubindu* fragment from Gilgit — by Klaus Wille

Among the Sanskrit fragments from the Gilgit finds of 1938 in the Sri Pratap Singh Museum (Srinagar)[17] I could identify in December 2010 one fragment as belonging to the *Hetubindu* of Dharmakīrti. My transliteration is based on two photographs taken during two visits of Chandrabhal Tripathi to the museum, one taken in 1982 and the other one in 1987. At that time the fragment was broken into two parts. The material is birch bark, the script Gilgit/Bāmiyān type II (= Proto-Śāradā) of the 7th to 8th centuries. The signature of this fragment given by Ch. Tripathi is A 16.

Postscript (Steinkellner): The floods of September 2014 also hit the Sri Pratap Singh Museum. By the end of October it was not yet known for sure whether its manuscript treasures were touched by the waters. It also seems to be uncertain whether the above described fragment is still among the museum's holdings.

---

[17] For this collection see Oskar von Hinüber, "The Gilgit Manuscripts: An Ancient Buddhist Library in Modern Research," in: P. Harrison and J.-U. Hartmann (eds), *From Birch Bark to Digital Data: Recent Advances in Buddhist Manuscript Research – Papers Presented at the Conference Indic Buddhist Manuscripts: The State of the Field, Stanford, June 15–19 2009.* (BKGA 80) Wien VÖAW 2014, pp. 79–135, especially 111 ff. For the history of the Sri Pratap Singh Museum see the homepage of the museum – spsmuseum.org – and, e.g., Ram Chandra Kak, *Handbook of the Archaeological and Numismatic Sections of the Sri Pratap Singh Museum, Srinagar*, Calcutta/Simla 1923. In earlier publications one finds the spelling Sir Pratap Singh Museum [cf. Oskar von Hinüber, "Die Erforschung der Gilgit-Handschriften (Funde buddhitischer Sanskrit-Handschriften, I)," *Nachrichten der Akademie der Wissenschaften in Göttingen* 1979, p. 329] and even on the labels with the signature on the photographs of the fragments this variant is written. But although the Maharaja's appellation is H.H. Sir Pratap Singh, the museum's name is Sri Pratap Singh Museum.

Some observations on the present edition

We know that the scribe or the corrector of the *Hetubindu* manuscript had at least one other manuscript at his disposal, and that the exemplar of the Tibetan translation seems to belong to a different transmission lineage, possibly that of the other manuscript. The conception of a hypothetical stemma, however, would be inappropriate under the present circumstances. Thus, the critical edition of the *Hetubindu* here offered is nothing but the edition of a copy of the ca. 13th century CE manuscript in the Potala the position of which within a stemma is still not determined, and the prospects for getting beyond this state are minimal at present.

The following sources are available: the Sanskrit texts of the *Hetubindu* Potala manuscript (ms, ca. 13th cent. CE) and the Srinagar fragment (msS, ca. 8th cent. CE), as well as of the commentaries *Hetubinduṭīkā* (HBṬ, ms, 11th or 12th cent. CE) and *Hetubinduṭīkāloka* (HBṬĀ, in "old Nevārī" script, after the 12th cent. CE), and the Tibetan translations of the *Hetubindu* (HB$_t$, ca. 800 CE), the *Hetubindutīkā* (HBṬ$_t$, ca. 800 CE), Vinītadeva's *Hetubinduṭīkā* (HBṬī$_t$, ca. 800 CE), and Śākyabuddhi's *Pramāṇavārttikaṭīkā* (PVṬ$_t$, 11th cent. CE).

Besides variants in the many paraphrases of Arcaṭa's *Ṭīkā*, there are also quite a number of variants in the edition's *pratīka*s. The Tibetan translations, although in general reliable as to the content of *pramāṇa* texts, notoriously deviate in many respects in terms of their linguistic form. It is, therefore, almost impossible to isolate instances that can be seen as definitely representing a Sanskrit variant in their exemplar.

The only case of some assertive value I found may be that of the variant °*patha*, Tib. *lam*, in contrast to °*viṣaya* of the manuscript (see below). Some support may also be drawn from the minor witnesses. Yet their transmission is usually hard to trace on the basis of the available modern editions. While, of course, it remains largely a matter of subjective opinion, I decided nevertheless to use my sigla for differentiating between more or less reliable witnesses, i.e., the **Ci** or

Ci' and the **Cie** or **Ci'e** type. The variants found in **Ci** and **Ci'** texts are recorded in a separate apparatus.

A few variants occur in the Srinagar fragment but are, I think, not sufficient for determining it as belonging to yet another line of transmission: msSa2 has *tasya* for *tasyāpi* ms, and msSa5 has *kevalaḥ* for *kevalo 'pi* ms. Here *api* is supported by Tib. *yaṅ*, even if *de'i ltar na* for *tasya* is unusual but not impossible. More substantial are the following two variants: *akṣepakriyāsvabhāvaḥ* msSa6 (*mi sdod par skyed pa'i chos can ṅo bo ñid* T, PVṬ$_t$) for *akṣepakriyādharmā svabhāvaḥ* ms12a2; cf. HBṬ 125, 19), and *ātmanaḥ* (msSb1, Utp, *bdag ñid kyi* T; cf. HBṬ 126,25) for *sātmanaḥ* ms 12a3.

The thorough edition based on the Peking and Derge versions of the lengthy excerpt from the *Hetubindu* in the *Pramāṇavārttikaṭīkā* which Koji Ezaki meritoriously sent to Krasser is also of interest in this connection. The PVṬ$_t$ was translated by rMa dGe ba'i blo gros. One would expect considerable differences in the translation, but the excerpt in question impresses me as quite a faithful copy of the *Hetubindu*'s translation by Prajñāvarman and dPal brtsegs rakṣita. Except for numerous differences in spellings and gaps due to eyeskips or sloppiness, as well as some wrongly introduced negations, there are, however, at least two valuable readings in this excerpt: *gnas skabs de gñis dṅos po tha dad par* (P 169a4, D 144a7) for *gnas skabs de gñis po tha dad par* (HB$_t$ 44,28) (*tayor avasthayor vastubhedaḥ* ms), and *mi 'bad do* (P 170a3, D 145a7) for *mi 'dod do* (HB$_t$ 48, 23–24) (*na nirbandhaḥ* ms).[18]

But this excerpt also bears the variant *lam* as found in HB$_t$, which provides support for the assumption that the excerpt was copied from Prajñāvarman's and dPal brtsegs' translation. Vinītadeva's *Hetubinduṭīkā*, translated by the same team, also has *lam* (HBṬī$_t$ 166a1). The reading *lam* in these three Tibetan translations (HB$_t$, HBṬī$_t$, PVṬ$_t$), all earlier than the Potala Sanskrit manuscript, is incidentally corroborated

[18] *'bad* for *'dod* has already been conjectured in Yoshimizu 2003: 214.

by the scribe or the corrector of the manuscript when he mentions °*pathaḥ* as a variant for °*viṣayam*: *patha iti kvacit pāṭhaḥ* (11a1, marg. above line 1+1).[19] The scribe or corrector, then, had access to one further manuscript whose congruence with the readings attested through the earlier Tibetan translations may indicate that these belong to the lineage of that second manuscript.

A number of cases may possibly be in opposition to this assumption, cases where the exemplar of the Tibetan translation – if accepted as truly representing its exemplar – would differ from the exemplar from which the corrections in the manuscript derive. I am grateful to Cristina Pecchia for bringing this fact to my attention.

27,1: ‹*pakṣe*› n.e. T; 29,8: ‹*dṛṣṭam*› n.e. T; 34,10: ‹*na*› n.e. T[20]; 34,11: ‹*anyatra*› n.e. T; 35,15: ‹*eva*› n.e. T; *a*‹*yaṃ*› n.e. T; 36,15: ‹*vyavahāra*› n.e. T; 38,15: ‹*anyatra*› n.e. T

Index

A KWIC (Key Word In Context) index of HB$_{St}$ is included in Ono/Oda/Takashima 1996. More or less all important terms can be found there and via the edition of HB$_{St}$. Then they can easily be traced in the present edition by means of the paragraphs which are left almost unchanged.

Conventions for the critical edition

Punctuation is editorial. The marks used are *daṇḍa*, double *daṇḍa*, dashes, and commas. Division into sections and paragraphs is editorial. Indistinguishable *akṣara*s (such as

[19] The only other variant indicated in this way is *kṣiṇoti* for *dunoti* (*kṣiṇotīti kvacit*, 11a2, marg. above lines 1 and 2). But since *gduṅ ba* may translate both verbs, this variant has no value for assessing the reading in the exemplar of the Tibetan translations.

[20] This *na* I consider as an actually superfluous gloss.

ba/va) have been read according to expectation. The classical rules of sandhi have been applied.

The following peculiarities of the manuscript are not recorded:

1. Regular geminations of *g, t, n, m, v* after °*r,* as well as degemination of *t* before *v*°
2. Non-application of classical sandhi rules
3. Use of class sibilant before a sibilant instead of *visarga*; use of *anusvāra* for homorganic nasal or the reverse, and *in pausa*
4. Omission of *avagraha*
5. Lack of *virāma*
6. Gaps between *akṣara*s

Marginal notes in the critical edition

Inner margin: line numbers and, in bold script, references to the analytic survey.

Outer margin: references to the manuscript, to the Srinagar fragment, to the Tibetan translation in HB_{St}, and to the *Hetu-binduṭīkā*.

Notes on the apparatuses

There are four apparatuses: 1. Minor witnesses, 2. Marginalia in the manuscript, 3. Critical apparatus, 4. Variant readings in minor witnesses.

The first apparatus contains the minor witnesses hitherto identified. Their position in the text is marked by pairs of superscript letters in repeated alphabets ([a]text[a]). Words and phrases commented on in Arcaṭa's HBṬ or Durvekamiśra's HBṬĀ, except for evident citations, are not indicated. This was done in the reconstruction of HB_{St} for obvious reasons. Here, however, reference to these two commentaries is limited to such texts which can also be considered minor witnesses properly speaking, that is, to citations referred to before or after the commenting sections. These references are given at the beginning of entries. In case they display changes, “cf.” is added.

The second apparatus contains all texts that appear in the margin of the manuscript and do not belong to the text of the *Hetubindu*. They are considered glosses. Like the additions to be inserted into the text, these marginal notes are usually also accompanied by cyphers referring to the lines of the text below or above, and their place of reference is mostly indicated in the lines by one or two signs of insertion (*kākapāda*s). The position of these marginalia is indicated in the diplomatic edition. In the critical edition, the point of insertion of the marginal text is marked by a capital (A, etc.) above the word referred to. If neither a cypher for the line nor an insertion sign are visible, the insertion is only conjectured on the basis of the context.

The third apparatus is the critical one. References are made to the lines of the text page above, where a superscript asterisk* indicates the place referred to. Multiple references to the same line are separated by ››. This apparatus is positive and begins with the accepted form. Arguments in support are added in parentheses. Forms of words written differently in the manuscript are indicated without repetition of the accepted form in the edited text.

Deviating from my policy in PVin 1–2: xli–xlii, I also included variants from minor witnesses judged as **Ci** or **Ci'** texts. The fourth apparatus contains these variant readings. References in the text are marked by superscript Greek letters, $^{\alpha}$ etc. Accidental errors by the scribes or editors are not noted. All variants occurring in minor witnesses judged as **Cie** and **Ci'e** texts are also not noted.

Editorial signs and sigla

In the critical edition

A etc. indicates the location of the marginalia as referred in the manuscript

[a]text[a] contains text referred to in the apparatus of minor witnesses

$^{\alpha}$ etc. indicates variants in minor witnesses

* indicates the record of variants in the critical apparatus

bold type highlights words from the programmatic stanza

underlined are names, references to persons, schools or texts

General abbreviations

add.	added
cf.	confer
em.	emended
gl.	gloss
marg.	marginal note
ms	the Potala manuscript of the *Hetubindu*
msS	the Srinagar fragment of the *Hetubindu*
n.e.	no equivalent in
om.	omitted
T	Tibetan translation of the *Hetubindu* as edited in HB_{St}
v.l.	varia lectio

Signs in the diplomatic and critical editions

â ā written as upper hook

âu au written as upper hook

ê e written as superscript

ô o partly written as superscript

t' specific t in final position[19]

t* ta with *virāma*

t⁰ ta without *virāma* where it is expected

* *virāma*

¦ deleted *daṇḍa* or dots as filling sign (at the end of lines or before string hole square)

‡ filling sign

□ empty space of one *akṣara*

n? uncertain reading

n! sic!

/ separates alternatives

[nn] content difficult to read

•• / • unreadable or unidentifiable *akṣara* or part of an *akṣara*

⊙ square space for binding hole

/// leaf broken off here

‹nn› content added in the line or margin

‸ / ˇ / ˇ‸ *kākapāda*s

{nn} content deleted by small stroke(s) or erasure

<nn> content emended

| *daṇḍa*

|| double *daṇḍa*

---

[19] Called *khaṇḍa-ta* in the Bengālī script.

ˡ	small secondary *daṇḍa* above the line
ˌ	small secondary *daṇḍa* below the line
॥| |॥	small secondary double *daṇḍa* to the right or left of a *daṇḍa* or double *daṇḍa*
~	sign for *siddham*
‖ o ‖	specific sequence of signs that marks the end of a section

Sigla for types of minor witnesses[20]

Ce *citatum ex alio* / citation from another text marked as such

Ce' *citatum ex alio usus secundarii* / citation from another text used secondarily and not marked as citation

Cee *citatum ex alio modo edendi* / citation from another text marked as such, with redactional changes

Ce'e *citatum ex alio usus secundarii modo edendi* / citation from another text not marked as citation, with redactional changes

Ci *citatum in alio* / citation in another text

Ci' *citatum in alio usus secundarii* / citation in another text not marked as citation and used secondarily

Cie *citatum in alio modo edendi* / citation in another text with redactional changes

Ci'e *citatum in alio usus secundarii modo edendi* / citation in another text used secondarily and not marked as citation, with redactional changes

Re' *relatum ex alio* / content reported from another text used secondarily

[20] Cf. Steinkellner 1988 for the usefulness of this system of differentiation.

The Srinagar fragment

The Potala manuscript

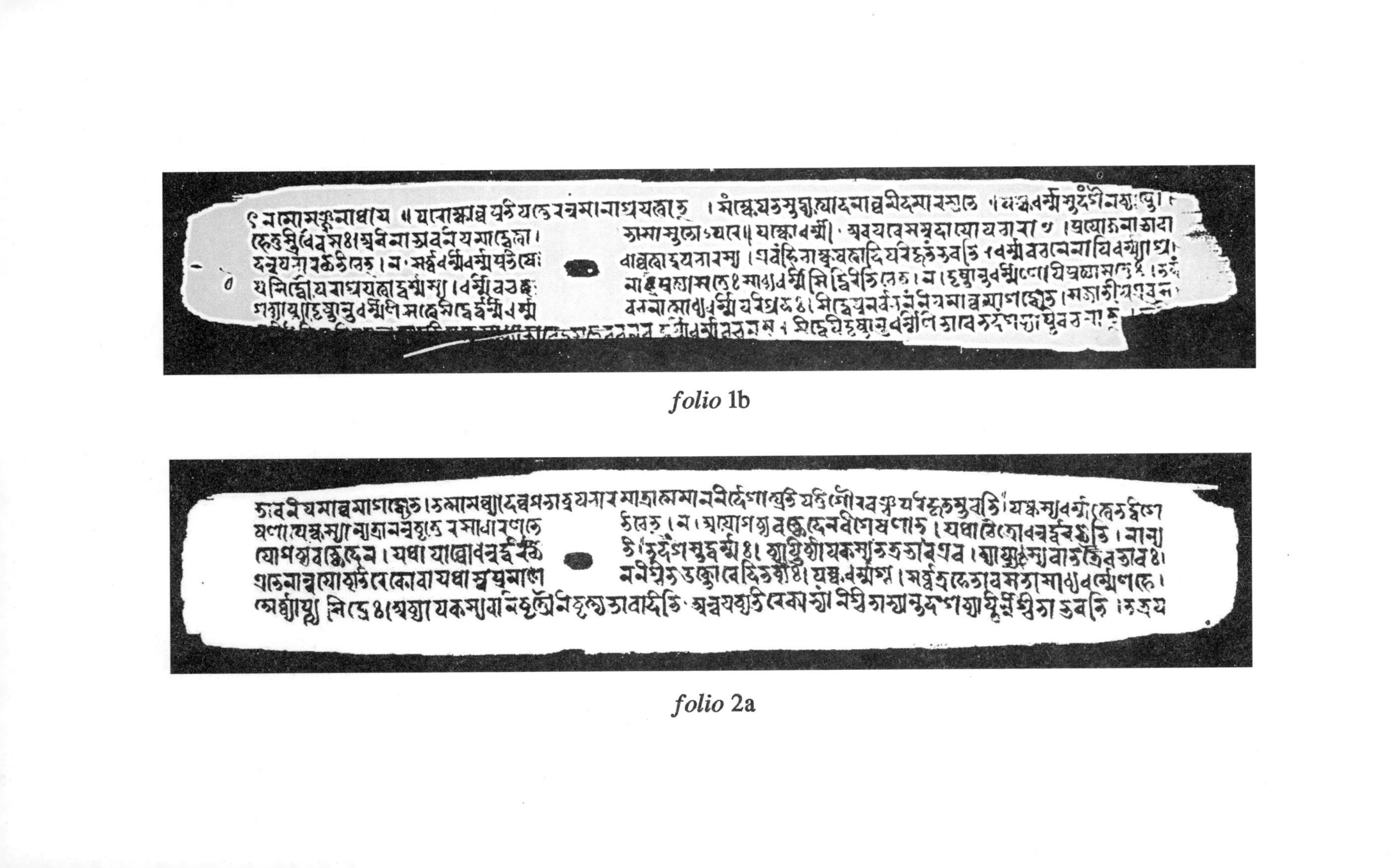

folio 1b

folio 2a

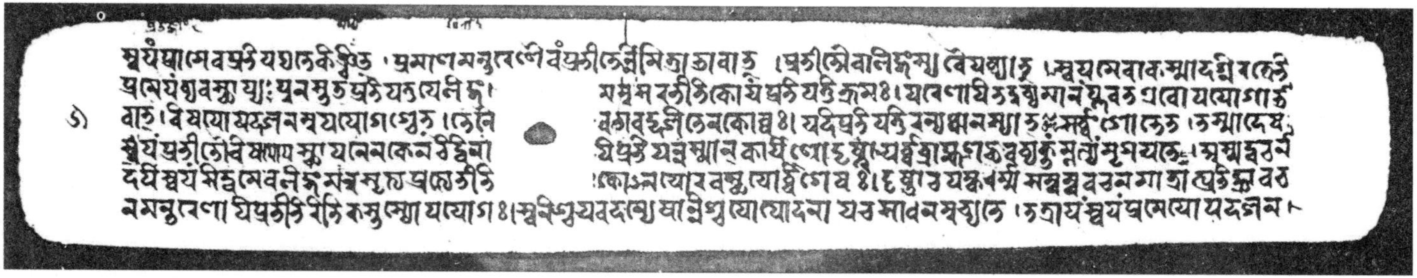

folio 5b

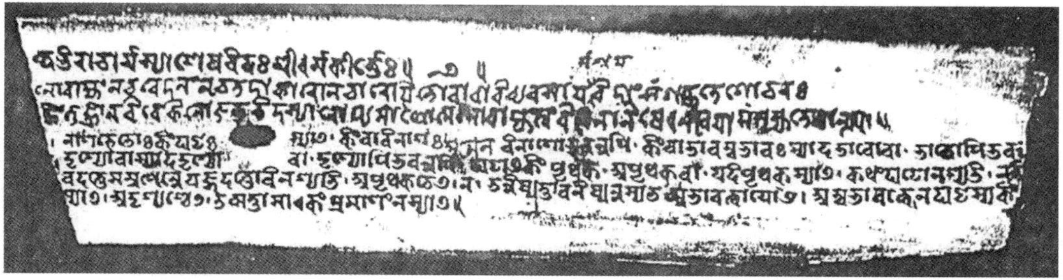

folio 25b

Critical Edition

0. [1] ~ नमो मञ्जुनाथाय ॥ ms 1b

0.1 परोक्षार्थप्रतिपत्तेरनुमानाश्रयत्वात् सङ्क्षेपतस् तद्व्युत्पादनार्थमिदमारभ्यते ॥ T 30,5

0.2 [ab]पक्षधर्मस् तदंशेन व्याप्तो [2]हेतुस्[b] त्रिधैव सः ।
अविनाभावनियमाद् धेत्वाभासास् ततो ऽपरे[a] ॥

1./1.1 [cd]पक्षो धर्मी,[d] अवयवे समुदायोपचरात्। [ef]प्रयोजनाभावा[3]दनुपचार HBṬ 11,20
इति चेत्, न, सर्वधर्मिधर्मप्रतिषेधार्थत्वादुपचारस्य। एवं हि चाक्षुष-
त्वादि परिहृतं भवति[f]। धर्मवचनेनापि धर्म्याश्र[4]यसिद्धौ पराश्रयत्वाद्
धर्मस्य धर्मिवचनात्[*] प्रत्यासत्तेः साध्यधर्मिसिद्धिरिति चेत्, न[*], दृष्टा-
न्तधर्मिणो ऽपि प्रत्यासत्तेः[e]। तदं[5]शव्याप्त्या दृष्टान्तधर्मिणि [*]सत्त्व- HBṬ 13,6
सिद्धेर्धर्मिधर्मवचनात् साध्यधर्मिपरिग्रहः। सिद्धे[*] पुनर्वचनं नियमा-
र्थमाशङ्क्येत। [g]सजातीय एव सत्त्वमि[g]ति[*] सिद्धे ऽपि तदभावे व्यतिरेके
[h]सा[6]ध्याभावे[*] ऽसत्त्व[h]वचनवद् धर्मिधर्मवचनं सिद्धे ऽपि दृष्टान्तधर्मि-
णि भावे तदंशव्याप्तिवचनात् तत्रैव[*] [1]भावनियमार्थमाशङ्क्येत[*]। तत् ms 2a

---

a-a Ce' PV 1.1; Ci TBV 556,3–4; SAS 9,15   b-b Ce'e HMu? (cf. Frauwallner 1954: 144 n.10; 145 n.11)   c-c Ce'e PVSV 1,12–2,14   d-d cf. PVin 3.43,3   e-e cf. PVin 3.43,3–8   f-f Ci'e PSṬ 3.119a5–6; cf. PVA 580,18–20   g-g Tarkaśāstra (cf. HBṬ 13,18)   h-h Tarkaśāstra (cf. HBṬ 13,18)

---

9 kyaṅ add. T (commented on in HBṬṭ 127b8–128a3) » na n.e. T   10 sattva° em. : satve ms   11 grub kyaṅ T for siddhe   12 mthun pa la yod pa kho nas T for sajātīya eva sattvam iti   12–13 sa‹ttvam iti siddhe ’pi tadabhāve vyatireke› sādhyābhāve em. (mthun pa la yod pa kho nas ldog pa la de med par grub mod kyi bsgrub par bya ba med pa la T; cf. HBṬ 13, 20–21; PVSV 2,5–6) : sa•• •• •• •• •• •• •• •• •• •• •• •• •• ••dhyābhāve ms   14 tatraiva em. (HBṬ 14,1; de ñid la T) : •• •• •• ms » For a possible connection of the sentence sajatīya eva ... asattvavacanat with the previous one and the deletion of the remaining dharmidharmavacanaṃ ... āśaṅkyeta cf. Krasser 2014: 310–311.

सामर्थ्यादर्थगतावुपचारमात्रात् समाननिर्देशात् प्रतिपत्तिगौरवं च
परिहृतं भवति। पक्षस्य धर्मत्वे तद्विशे$_2$षणापेक्षस्यान्यत्राननुवृत्तेरसा- 1.2
धारणतेति चेत्, [ij]न, अयोगव्यवच्छेदेन विशेषणात्[j], [k]यथा चैत्रो धनु-
र्धर इति[i], नान्य$_3$योगव्यवच्छेदेन, यथा पार्थो धनुर्धर[k] इति॥

HBṬ 17,20 **तदंशस्** तद्धर्मः॥ 2.

[l]व्याप्ति[m]र्व्यापकस्य तत्र भाव एव[m], व्याप्यस्य वा तत्रैव भावः[l]॥ 3.

T 32,11 $_4$एतेनान्वयो व्यतिरेको वा यथास्वं प्रमाणेन निश्चित उक्तो वेदित- 3.1
व्यः[*] पक्षधर्मश् च[c], सर्वत्र हेतावसता साध्यधर्मेण [*]हे$_5$तोर्व्याप्त्यसिद्धेः,
व्यापकस्य[*] वा निवृत्तौ निवृत्त्यभावादित्य[*]न्वयव्यतिरेकाभ्यां निश्चि-
ताभ्यां तदंशव्याप्तिर्निश्चिता भवति॥

ms 2b HBṬ 20,8 तत्र [n]प$_1$क्षधर्मस्य साध्यधर्मिणिप्रत्यक्षतोऽनुमानतो[*] वा प्रसिद्धिर्नि- 3.2
श्चयः,[n] यथा प्रदेशे धूमस्य शब्दे वा कृतकत्वस्य। [o]सधूमं हि प्रदेश-
मर्थान्तरवि$_2$विक्तरूपमसाधारणात्मना दृष्टवतः प्रत्यक्षेण यथादृष्ट-
भेद[A*]परमार्थविषयं स्मार्तं लिङ्गज्ञानमुत्पद्यते[o]॥

HBṬ 25,11 [pq]तत्र तदाद्यमसाधारणविष$_3$यं[q] दर्शनमेव[*] प्रमाणम्[p]॥ a.1

[i-i] **Ci'** PSṬ 2.35,7–8 [j-j] cf. PVin 2.50,7 [k-k] cf. DAṬ 2,8–10 [l-l] **Ci** NBṬ 155,1; **Cie** J 164,3 [m-m] HBṬ 62,20–21 [n-n] HBṬ 39,11–12; cf. TBV 76,34 [o-o] **Ci'e** PSṬ 2.34,5–7 [p-p] HBṬĀ 39,27; 40,1; **Ci'e** PSṬ 2.34,8 [q-q] **Ci** DhPr 75,18

[A] ‹yadā niścayaṃ janayati | tadaiva pramāṇaṃ |› gl. ms

7–8 veditavyaḥ n.e. T **8** hetoḥ n.e. T **9** vyāpakasya (khyab par byed pa T) : avyāpakasya ms » iti n.e. T **11** 'numānat{au}o ms **14** paramārtha n.e. T **15** mthoṅ ba gaṅ yin de kho na T for tad ... darśanam eva

a.2 तस्मिंस् तथाभूते दृष्टे स येन येनासाधारणस् तदसाधारणतां ततो (T 32,24) भेदमभिलपन्ती स्मृतिरुत्पन्ना प्रत्यक्ष[4]बलेनातद्व्यावृत्तिविषया यथादृष्टाकारग्रहणान् न प्रमाणम्, प्रागसाधारणं दृष्ट्वा ऽसाधारणमित्यभिलपतो ऽपूर्वार्थाधिगमाभा[5]वात्, अर्थक्रियासाधनस्य दर्शनात्, अदृष्टस्य तत्साधनस्य पुनः स्वभावस्य विकल्पेनाप्रतिपत्तेश् चानुमानवत्। [rs]अर्थक्रियाऽर्थी हि सर्वः[*] प्र[1]माणमप्रमाणं [α]वा[s] ऽन्वेषते प्रेक्षावान्[r]। (ms 3a) [tu]न च सामान्यं[*] काञ्चिदर्थक्रियामुपकल्पयति[u] [v]स्वलक्षणप्रतिपत्तेरूर्ध्वं[v] तत्सामर्थ्योत्पन्नवि[2]कल्पज्ञानग्राह्यम्[t], [w]यथा नीलं दृष्ट्वा नीलमिति ज्ञाने[*w]। तदेव हि नीलस्वलक्षणं तथाविधसाध्यार्थक्रियाकारि। तच् च (HBṬ 32,20) तेना[3]त्मना प्रत्यक्षेण दृष्ट[B]मेव। न च तत्स्वलक्षणग्रहणोत्तरकालभाविनो नीलविकल्पस्य विषयेण नीलसाध्यार्थक्रिया साध्य[4]ते। [xy]तस्माद् [z]अनधिगतार्थविषयं प्रमाणमि[yz]त्यप्य[a]नधिगते स्वलक्षण[a] इति विशेषणीयम्[x]। [b]अधिगते[β] स्वलक्षणे तत्सामर्थ्यजन्मा [5]विकल्पस् तदनुकारी कार्यतस् तद्विषयत्वात् स्मृतिरेव [c]न प्रमाणम्, अनधिगतवस्तुरूपानधिगतेः, [bcd]वस्त्वधिष्ठान[C]त्वात् प्रमाण[6]व्यवस्थायाः, [de]अर्थक्रि-

---

r-r **Ci** TSP² 489,23; **Ci'** TSP² 942,18–19; TR 2,11 s-s **Ci** NBhū 294,2 t-t **Ci** DAṬ 32,20–21 u-u **Cie** HBṬ 29,6–7; 33,8–9 v-v **Ci** HBṬĀ 281,7 w-w HBṬ 33,8; 38,22 x-x **Ci** DAṬ 32,8–9; **Cie** PPar II 4,15–17 y-y **Ci** PVinṬ(a) 9,14–16 z-z cf. PVin 1.20,1; **Ci'e** NBṬ 19,2 a-a **Ce'e** PV 2.6'b b-b **Ci** DAṬ 31,16–17 (cf. Jambūvijaya 1981: 134) c-c **Ci'e** PSṬ 2.34,7–8 d-d HBṬ 4,26; **Ci'** PSṬ 2.34,9–10 e-e HBṬ 35,19

B ‹adhyavasāyaṃ kurvat pratyakṣaṃ pramā•• ••› gl. ms (cf. tasmād adhyavasāyaṃ kurvad eva pratyakṣaṃ pramāṇaṃ bhavati NBṬ 84,5) C ‹rūpa› gl. ms

---

6 sarvva‹ḥ› ms **7** sāmānya<ṃ> em. (cf. DAṬ 32,20) : sāmānya ms **9** rnam par śes pa la snaṅ ba T for jñāne

---

α ca NBhū; TSP 489,23 for vā (TSP 942,19) β adhigate tu DAṬ for adhigate

यायोग्य[e]विषयत्वात् तदर्थि[*]प्रवृत्तेः, अर्थक्रियायोग्यलक्षणत्वाद् वस्तु-
ms 3b नः, [fg]ततो ऽपि विकल्पात् तद[D]ध्यवसायेन वस्तुन्येव [1]प्रवृत्तेः[g], प्रवृ-
त्तौ तु[*γ] विकल्पस्य[δ] प्रत्यक्षेणाभिन्नयोगक्षेमत्वात्[f] ॥

T 34,26 HBṬ 37,5 पूर्वप्रत्यक्षक्षणेन[*] क्वचिदभिन्नोपयोगत्वादुत्तरेषामप्रामाण्यप्रसङ्ग इति a.21
[2]चेत्, न, क्षणविशेषसाध्यार्थवाञ्छायां नानायोगक्षेमत्वात्। साधारणे
हि कार्ये न तेषां सामर्थ्यभेदः, [h]अपरापरधूम[3]प्रमितसन्निकृष्टाग्निवद्[h]-
ग्निमात्रसाध्ये ऽर्थे। एतेन धर्मिधर्मलिङ्गादिविकल्पस्य प्रमाणपृष्ठभावि- (a.2)
नः प्रामाण्यं प्रत्युक्तम्॥

HBṬ 41,5 [4][i]अन्वयनिश्चयो ऽपि स्वभावहेतौ[i] साध्यधर्मस्य [j]वस्तुतस् तद्भाव- 3.31
तया[j] साधनधर्मभावमात्रानुबन्धसिद्धिः। [k]सा साध्यविपर्यये हेतो[5]र्बाध-
कप्रमाणवृत्तिः[k], यथा यत् सत्, तत् क्षणिकमेव। अक्षणिकत्वे ऽर्थ-
क्रियाविरोधात् तल्लक्षणं वस्तुत्वं हीयत इति[*]।

HBṬ 45,4 [l]कार्यहेतौ का[6]र्यकारणभावसिद्धिः, यथेदम[m]स्योपलम्भ उपलब्धिल- 3.32
क्षणप्राप्तमनुपलब्धमु[*]पलभ्यते[m] सत्स्वप्यन्येषु हेतुष्व[ε]स्याभावे न भव-

---

[f-f] **Ci** TBV 468,17–18; **Cie** PPar II 4,10–12 [g-g] **Cie** NKaṇḍ 441,10–11; PVinṬ(a) 7,15–16 [h-h] **Cie** PPar II 28,13–14 [i-i] HBṬ 76,21–22 [j-j] HBṬ 43,27 [k-k] HBṬĀ 306,30 [l-l] **Ci** Utp 39,2–5 [m-m] **Ce'e** PVSV 22,2 (cf. AJP II 176,10–177,1)

[D] ‹svalakṣaṇa› gl. ms

---

1 °arthi° n.e. T **2–3** pravṛttau ‹tu› ms **4** °kṣaṇena n.e. T **12** iti n.e. T
14 sṅon mi dmigs pa T for anupalabdham (ms; HBṬ 45,12; PVSV; Utp)

[γ] pravṛttau ca (TBV) for pravṛttau ‹tu› ms (źugs nas T; źugs pa na yaṅ PPar II)
[δ] vikalpasya om. TBV [ε] hetuṣu om. Utp

तीति तद्भावे[ζ] $_{1}$भावो ऽभावे[η] ऽभावश् च, [η][E]प्रत्यक्षानुपलम्भसाधनः[θ] ms 4a [ɩ]कार्यकारणभावः[η], तस्य सिद्धिः। कार्यकारणभाव एव ह्यर्थान्तरस्यैवं[*] स्यात् – यत्र धूमः, $_{2}$तत्रावश्यमग्निरिति[κ]। अग्निभाव एव हि भावो धूमस्य तत्कार्यत्वमिति[ɩ]।

3.33 अनुपलब्धावप्यसद्व्यवहारस्योपलब्धिलक्षणप्राप्तानुपल$_{3}$ब्धिमात्रवृत्तिसाधनमन्वयनिश्चयः, निमित्तान्तराभावोपदर्शनात्॥

3.41 व्यतिरेकनिश्चयो ऽपि कार्यस्वभावहेत्वोः कार्यकारणव्याप्य$_{4}$व्यापक- T 36,23 HBṬ 51,8 भावसिद्धौ कारणव्यापकानुपलब्धिभ्यां दृश्यविषयाभ्यां साध्याभावे हेत्वभावसिद्धिः, उद्दिष्टविषयस्याभावस्योप$_{5}$दर्शने ऽनुपलब्धिलक्षणप्राप्तस्यान्यथा क्वचिदभावासिद्धेः। अनुद्दिष्टविषयं पुनः साध्याभावे ऽभावख्यापनं प्रतिबन्धमात्रसिद्धौ सि$_{1}$ध्यतीति न तत्र दृश्यविषयता- ms 4b ऽनुपलब्धेर्व्यतिरेकसाधने[*] ऽपेक्ष्यते॥

3.42 व्यतिरेकनिश्चयो ऽनुपलब्धावुपलब्धिलक्षणप्राप्तात् [*]सतोऽनुपलम्भा$_{2}$भावदर्शनम्[*]॥

4. एतल्लक्षणस् **त्रिधैव स** हेतुस् त्रिप्रकार एव – स्वभावः कार्यमनुपल- T 38,4 HBṬ 54,22 ब्धिश् चेति, यथाऽनित्ये कस्मिंश्चिद्गम्ये[*] सत्त्वम$_{3}$ग्निमति प्रदेशे धूमो ऽभावे[F] चोपलब्धिलक्षणप्राप्तस्यानुपलब्धिरिति, अस्मिन्नेव त्रिप्रकारे

η-η Ci AJP II 176,7; 187,10; Ci TBV 96,28–29

E ‹trividhaḥ› gl. ms F ‹abhāvavyavahāre› gl. ms

---

3 kho nar T for evam 12 ldog pa bsgrub par bya ba la T for vyatirekasādhane 13 sataḥ n.e. T 14 ñe bar ston pa T for °darśanam* 16 bsgrub par bya ba la T for gamye

---

ζ yas tadbhāve Utp for tadbhāve η tadabhāve Utp for abhāve θ °sādhanaṃ TBV for °sādhanaḥ ɩ kārya° om. Utp κ agniḥ Utp for agnir iti

ऽविनाभावनियमात्। यथो[4]क्ता व्याप्तिरविनाभावः पक्षधर्मस्य। [o]न स
त्रिविधाद् धेतोरन्यत्रास्तीत्यत्रैव नियत उच्यते[o]॥

HBṬ 57,3 तत्र [p]साधनधर्मभावमात्रान्वयिनि[p] साध्य[5]धर्मे स्वभावो हेतुः। व- 4.10 4.111
स्तुतो लिङ्गिस्वभाव एवापरापरव्यावृत्त्या धर्मभेदे ऽपि हेतुः। हेतुस्व- 4.112
ms 5a भावे* ऽन्वयव्यभिचाराभावाद् विशेषणं लक्षणे [1]तन्मात्रान्वयेन परम-
तापेक्षम्। परे ह्यर्थान्तरनिमित्तम[q]तद्भावमात्रान्वयिनमपि धर्मं स्वभा-
वमिच्छन्ती[q]ति विशेषणेन तथाविधस्या[r]*तत्स्वभावतां [2]तस्मिन् साध्ये
हेतोर्व्यभिचारं चाह, यथा विनाशे हेतुमति कृतकत्वस्य[r]॥

HBṬ 61,24 तस्य द्विधा प्रयोगः, साधर्म्येण वैधर्म्येण च, यथा – य[3]त् सत्, तत् 4.12
सर्वं क्षणिकम्, यथा घटादयः। संश्‌ च शब्द इति। तथा – क्षणिक-
त्वाभावे सत्त्वाभावः, यथा वन्ध्यासुते*। संश्‌ च शब्द इति [4]सर्वोपसं-
हारेणान्वयेन व्यतिरेकेण च* व्याप्तिप्रदर्शनलक्षणौ साधर्म्यवैधर्म्यप्र-
योगौ॥

T 38,32 अत्र सामर्थ्यादेव प्रतिज्ञार्थ[5]प्रतीतेर्न प्रतिज्ञाप्रयोगः। अप्रदर्शिते प्र- 4.131
मेये* कथं तत्प्रतीतिरिति चेत्, स्वयं प्रतिपत्तौ कः प्रमेयस्य दर्शयि-
ता*। प्रदे[6]शस्थं धूममुपलब्धवतस् तस्याग्निना व्याप्तिस्मरणे तत्साम-

---

o-o HBṬ 8,1–2; Ci TBV 558,30–31 p-p HBṬ 57,17 q-q HBṬ 58,20 r-r cf. HBṬ 61,22

4–5 'pi <hetuḥ> | hetusvabhāve em. (cf. gtan tshigs ni rtags can gyi raṅ bźin kho na yin no ‖ T) : 'pi | hetusvabhāve ms (cf. HBṬ 57,19–20 supporting the component hetusvabhāve) (I assume here a case of haplography) **7** °tat° n.e. T **11** yathā vandhyāsute n.e. T **12** {vā} ca ms **14–15** gźal bya'i don T for prameye **15–16** ñe bar ston par byed pa T for darśayitā

थ्यादेवाग्निरत्रेति भवति[*]। न च तत्र कश्चिदग्निरत्रेत्यस्मै निवेदयति। नापि [1]स्वयं प्रागेव[*] प्रतिपद्यते किञ्चित्, प्रमाणमन्तरेणैवं प्रतीतेर्निमित्ताभावात्, (ms 5b) प्रतीतौ वा[*] लिङ्गस्य वैयर्थ्यात्। स्वयमेवाकस्मादग्निरत्रेति [2]प्रमेयं[G] व्यवस्थाप्य पुनस् तत्प्रतिपत्तये [*]लिङ्गमनुसरतीति को ऽयं प्रतिपत्तिक्रमः। परेणापि तदुच्यमानं प्लवत एव, उपयोगाभा[3]वात्॥

[s]विषयोपदर्शनमुपयोगश् चेत्[s], [t]तेनैव तावद् दर्शितेन[t] को ऽर्थः। (HBṬ 66,1) [u]यदि प्रतिपत्तिर[^]न्यथा न स्यात्, सर्वं शोभेत[u]। तस्मादेष [4]स्वयं प्रतीतौ विषयोपस्थापनेन केनचिद् विनापि [v]प्रतियन्नस्मान् कार्यिणो दृष्ट्वा पर्वब्राह्मण इव व्यक्तं मूल्यं मृगयते[v]। अस्मद्वचना[5]दपि स्वयं सिद्धमेव लिङ्गमनुसृत्य प्रत्येतीति को ऽनयोरवस्थयोर्विशेषः। [w]दृष्टा च पक्षधर्मसम्बन्धवचनमात्रात् प्रतिज्ञावच[6]नमन्तरेणापि प्रतीतिरिति कस् तस्योपयोगः[w]। स्वनिश्चयवदन्येषां निश्चयोत्पादनाय च साधनमुच्यते, तत्रायं स्वयं प्रमेयोपदर्शन[1]मन्तरेणापि प्रतिपद्य[*] परं प्रतिपादयन्नपूर्व- (ms 6a) मर्थक्रममाश्रयत इति किमत्र कारणम्। तस्मान् न प्रमेयवचनेन किञ्चित्, [x]अन्यथापि [*]तत्प्रतिप[2]त्तेरुत्पत्तेरि[x]ति॥

4.132 एतेनोपनयनिगमनादिकमपि प्रत्युक्तम्, एतावतैव[H] प्रयोगेण प्रतीतिभावादिति[*] (T 40,28; HBṬ 70,9) [yz]डिण्डिकरागं परित्यज्या[3]क्षिणी निमील्य चिन्तय

s-s cf. PV 4.21 t-t HBṬĀ 320,15 u-u **Ci** TBV 67,30–31 v-v cf. NBhū 285,8 w-w **Ci** TBV 67,31–32; cf. PV 4.22 x-x HBṬ 70,9 y-y PMim 57,27–28 z-z Vyom II 207,7–8; NM II 577,2–4; **Ci'e** NBhū 285,10–11

G ‹prat•jñām› gl. ms H ‹dvyavayavavākyenaiva› gl. ms

1 yod do sñam du śes so T for bhavati 2 eva n.e. T 3 vā n.e. T 4 yan lag T for liṅgam 13 rtogs la T for pratipadya 15 ‹tat›pratipatter ms 17 iti n.e. T

^ pratītir TBV (HBṬ 66,23) for pratipattir

तावत् – किमियता[l] प्रतीतिः स्यान्[μ] न वे[z]ति। भावे वा[*] किं प्रपञ्चमालये[y]तीयानेव साधनवाक्यप्रयोगो ज्यायान्[4] ॥

4.14 HBṬ 72,24 अत्रापि न कश्चित् पक्षधर्मसम्बन्धवचनप्रयोग[*]क्रम[*]नियमः, सर्वथा[*] गमकत्वात् ॥

4.15 T42,7 सम्बन्धवचने ऽपि प्रयोग एव[*] भिद्यते नार्थः[*], उ[5]भयथा धर्मभेदे ऽपि [a]तद्भावस्यैव ख्यापनात्[a]। [b]न [*]ह्येकान्तेनातत्स्वभावस्य भावे ऽन्यभावः[b], कृतकत्वभाव इव प्रयत्नोत्प[6]त्तिधर्मतायाः। नाप्यतत्स्वभावस्य निवृत्तौ तन्निवृत्तिरकार्यस्य, यथानयोरेव धर्मयोर्विपर्ययेण। [c]तस्मादन्वयव्यतिरेकयोर्यथालक्ष[1]णमे[ν]को ऽपि प्रयुक्तो[ξ] द्वितीयमा[o]क्षिपतीति[c] (ms 6b) नैकत्र साधनवाक्ये द्वयोः[J] प्रयोग इष्यते, वैयर्थ्यात्, तत्स्वभावतया [*]तदन्वयसिद्धौ तदभावे[2] ऽभावसिद्धेः, तदभावे ऽभावसिद्धौ च [*]तदन्वयसिद्धेः ॥

4.151 [d]तदभाव एवाभावख्यातिर्यथा स्यान् नान्यत्र न विरुद्ध इति नियमख्यापना[3]र्थो ऽपि व्यतिरेकप्रयोगो[d] न युक्तः, अन्यविरुद्धयोरपि विपक्षत्वात् ॥

---

a-a HBṬ 73,16   b-b HBṬ 73,33   c-c cf. PVin 2.52,12–13; TR 51,7–8   d-d cf. HBṬ 75,7–9

---

l ‹pakṣadharmasambandhavacanamātrakeṇa› gl. ms   J ‹anvayavyatirekayoḥ› gl. ms

---

1 vā n.e. T   3 vacana{yoḥ}‹prayoga›krama° ms » °prayoga° n.e. T » ji ltar yaṅ T for sarvathā   5 'ba' źig T for eva » nārthaḥ n.e. T   6 hi n.e. T   10 tad° n.e. T   11 tad° n.e. T

μ arthapratipattir bhavati NBhū for pratītiḥ syāt   ν niścitavyāptikayor TR for yathālakṣaṇam   ξ ekam api prayuktam TR for eko 'pi prayuktaḥ   o dvitīyam om. TR

b. कथमिदानीं* गम्यते सतो ऽवश्यं नश्वरः स्वभाव इति येनान्वयव्य[4]- T 42,24 HBṬ 76,3
b.1 तिरेकौ स्याताम्। विनाशहेत्वयोगात्। स्वभावत एव भावा नश्वराः।

b.11/b.111 नैषां निष्पन्नानामन्यतो नाशोत्पत्तिः, तस्यासामर्थ्यात्। न हि [5]वि-
b.112 नाशहेतुर्भावस्वभावमेव करोति, तस्यान्यतो* ऽभिनिर्वृत्तेः। [e]नापि स्व-
भावान्तरकरणे [f]तदवस्थस्य भावस्य* किञ्चिदिति तथोपलब्ध्यादिप्र-
सङ्गः[e]। [6][g]नापि स्वभावान्तरमस्यावरणम्, तदवस्थे तस्मिन्नावरण-
b.113 स्याप्ययोगात्[g]। [h]नापि विनाशहेतुना भावाभावः क्रियते[h], अभावस्य
विधिना *कार्य[1]त्वोपगमे व्यतिरेकाव्यतिरेकविकल्पानतिक्रमात्। भा- ms 7a
वप्रतिषेधरूपत्वे* च भावं न करोतीति स्यात्। तथा *चाकर्तुरहेतुत्व-
मिति न विनाशहे[2]तुः कश्चित्[f]॥

b.12/b.121 [i]वैयर्थ्याच् च। [j]यदि स्वभावतो नश्वरो भावः, तस्य न किञ्चिन् नाश- T 44,10 HBṬ 82,24
हेतुना, स्वयं तत्स्वभावतयैव नाशात्। [kl]यो हि* यस्य स्वभा[3]वः*, स स्व-
हेतोरेवोत्पद्यमानस् तादृशो भवति, न पुनस् तद्भावे* हेत्वन्तरमपेक्षते[l]
प्रकाशद्रवोष्णकठिनादिद्रव्यवत्[π]। न हि प्रकाशादय[4]स् तदात्मान
उत्पन्नाः पुनः प्रकाशादिभावे* हेत्वन्तरमपेक्षन्ते,[j] तदात्मनस् तादा-

---

e-e cf. PV 1.269cd; PVSV 142,8–9 f-f **Ci'e** PVṬ$_t$ Je,168b4–6 g-g cf. PV 1.271ab h-h cf. PVSV 142,10–17 (PV 1.270ab) i-i **Ci'** PVṬ$_t$ Je,168b6–169a2 j-j **Ci'e** TSP[2] 176,24–177,4; NBhū 526,14–17 k-k **Cie** Utp 75,5–8 l-l HBṬ 117,4–5; 138,18–20

---

1 'di T for idānīm **4** anyataḥ n.e. T **5** ‹tadava›sthasya ‹bhāvasya› ms
8 kāryatvo° n.e. T **9** ṅo bo ñid gcig yin na T for °rūpatve » ca n.e. T
12 hi n.e. T » ṅo bo ñid T for svabhāvaḥ **13** ṅo bor bya ba la T for bhāve
15 ṅo bor bya ba'i phyir T for bhāve

π °kaṭhinadravyādivat Utp for °kaṭhinādidravyavat

त्म्याभावे नैरात्म्यप्रसङ्गात्। तद्वदस्थितिधर्मा चेत् स्वभा[5]वतो भावो निष्पन्नः पुनर्न[ρ] तदात्मतायां[σ] हेत्वन्तरमपेक्षे[τ]त[ik] ॥

T 44,22 HBṬ 83,15 [Km]बीजादिवदनेकान्त इति चेत्, स्यादे[L]तत् – [n]बीजादयो ऽङ्कुरादेर्जननस्व[6]भावाः सन्तो ऽपि[*] न केवला जनयन्ति, सलिलादिकारणान्तरापेक्षत्वात्, तद्वद् भावो ऽपि विनाशे[*] स्यादिति[*n]। न, [o]तत्स्वभावस्य (ms 7b) जननादजनकस्य चा[u]त[1]त्स्वभावत्वात्[o]। [p]अत एव तयोरवस्थयोर्वस्तुभेदो[*] निश्चेयः[p], भावानां स्वभावान्यथात्वाभावात् तत्स्वभावस्य [q]पश्चादिव प्रागपि जननप्रसङ्गात्[q]। तस्माद् यो[2]ऽन्त्यो ऽवस्थाभेदः, स एवाङ्कुरादिजननस्वभावः। पूर्वभाविनस् त्ववस्थाविशेषाः[*] कारणकारणानीति[*] नानेकान्तः[*], [r]क्षणिकेषु भावेष्व[M]पराप[3]रोत्पत्तेरैक्याभावात्[mr] ॥ b.122

T 46,5 HBṬ 89,6 [st][*]ते ऽन्त्याःसमर्थाः किं न जनयन्ती[s]ति चेत्, [u]जनयन्त्येव[u], नात्रान्यथाभावः, स्वभावावैपरीत्यात्॥ b.12211

---

m-m Ci' PVṬ$_t$ Je,169a2–5 n-n cf. TSP² 177,5–7 o-o Cie VNṬ 7,18–19; HBṬ 117,3–4; 138,18 p-p HBṬ 117,9 q-q HBṬ 92,11 r-r HBṬ 133,29–30 s-s HBṬ 92,1 t-t Ci' PVṬ$_t$ Je,169a6–169b1 u-u HBṬ 89,24; 92,2–3

K ‹atra paraḥ prāha |› gl. ms L ‹siddhāntavādī prāha› gl. ms M ‹niranta-ragatya•ā› gl. ms

---

4 raṅ bźin yaṅ T for svabhāvāḥ santo ’pi **5** dṅos po ’jig pa yaṅ T for bhāvo ’pi vināśe » For a possible deletion of this clarification of the objection (syād etat ... syād iti) cf. Krasser 2014: 311. **6–7** tha dad par T for vastubhedaḥ **9** sṅon gyi gnas skabs na yod pa’i bye brag rnams ni T for pūrvabhāvinas tv avasthāviśeṣāḥ **9–10** rgyu’i rgyu ñid yin pas T for kāraṇakāraṇānīti **10** ma ṅes pa ñid yin no T for nānekāntaḥ **12** te n.e. T

ρ na punas Utp for niṣpannaḥ punar na σ tadātmatayā Utp for tadātmatāyām τ apekṣate Utp for apekṣeta υ kāraṇād akārakasya vā VNṬ for jananād ajanakasya ca

b.12212 तेषु सर्वेषु सह[4]कारिषु समर्थस्वभावेषु को ऽपरस्योपयोग इति चेत्, न वै भावानां काचित् प्रेक्षापूर्वकारिता, यतः – [v]अयमेको ऽपि[v] समर्थः किम[5]त्रास्माभिरित्यपरे निवर्तेरन्। ते हि[*] निरभिप्रायव्यापाराः स्वहेतुपरिणामोपनिधिधर्माणस् तत्प्रकृतेस् तथाभवन्तो नोपालम्भमर्ह[6]न्ति॥

b.12213 [w]समर्थाः[φ] किं नापरापरं जनयन्तीति चेत्, न, [x]तत्रैवैकत्र[*][χ] सामर्थ्यात्[x], [y]तस्यैवैकस्य जनने समर्था नान्यस्येति[ψ] [z]नापरापरजननम्[twyz]॥

b.12214 [abc]भिन्नस्व[1]भावेभ्यश्[ω] चक्षुरादिभ्यःसहकारिभ्य एककार्योत्पत्तौ न कारणभेदात् कार्यभेदः स्यादि[c]ति चेत्, न, यथास्वं स्वभावभेदेन तद्विशेषोपयोग[2]तः, तदुपयोगकार्य[α]स्वभाव[*]विशेषासङ्करात्[b]। [d]यथा मृत्पिण्डकुलालसूत्रादिभ्यो भवतो घटस्य [ef]मृत्पिण्डादमृत्स्वभावेभ्यो वृक्षादिभ्यो[f] [3]भिन्नः स्वभावः कुलालात् तस्यैव मृदात्मनः सतः संस्थानविशेषात्मतया तदन्येभ्यो भिन्नः सूत्रात् तस्यैव मृत्संस्थानविशेषात्मनश्[β] [γ]च[4]क्रादेर्विभक्तः स्वभावो[δ] भवति। [g]तदेवं न कुला- T 46,19 ms 8a HBṬ 92,15

---

v-v cf. HBṬ 126,127 w-w **Ci** Utp 15,8–9 x-x HBṬ 94,5; **Ci** AJP II 174,12 y-y HBṬ 93,8–9 z-z **Ci** AJP II 174,12–175,1 a-a **Ci'** PVṬ$_t$ Je,169b1–6; **Cie** Utp 42,13; 42,14–43,4 b-b **Cie** AJP II 174,7–9 c-c cf. AJP II 150,9–10; 154,5–6; 174,12 d-d **Ci'e** NBhū 522,8–11 e-e **Ci'e** Utp 43,5–7 f-f cf. NBhū (**Ci** J 25,10) g-g **Cie** Utp 43,11

---

3 te hi n.e. T **6** ekatra n.e. T **11** °svabhāva° n.e. T

φ te samarthāḥ Utp for samarthāḥ χ ekatra om. Utp ψ nānyasya om. Utp ω tena bhinnasvabhāvebhyaḥ Utp for bhinnasvabhāvebhyaḥ α tadupayogaḥ, kārya° Utp for tadupayogakārya° β °ātmakasyasataś Utp 43,6 for °ātmanaḥ γ cakrādibhiḥ Utp 43,2 for cakrādeḥ δ vibhaktasvabhāvo Utp 43,6 for vibhaktaḥ svabhāvaḥ

लान् मृत्स्वभावता न मृदः संस्थानविशेषः[gde] । [h]न च[*] तयोः शक्तिविशेषविषयभेदे ऽपि तज्ज[5]नितविशेषभेदस्य कार्यस्य स्वभावभेदः, [i]मृत्संस्थानयोरपरस्परात्मतया संस्थानमृत्स्वभाव[ε]विशेषाभ्यां[*] तयोरप्रतिभासनप्रसङ्गात्[ahi] ॥

T 48,7 ms 8b HBṬ 107,25 [N jk]अन्य[1]देव संस्थानं गुणो [*]मृद्द्रव्यात्। तेन भिन्नः स्वभावः[*ζ] कुलालमृत्पिण्ड[*]योरुपयोगविषय इति चेत्, उक्तमत्र। अपि च[η] यदि [*]तत्संस्थानं भिन्नं मृदः, कु[2]लालः किं न पृथक् करोति[j]। गुणस्य द्रव्यपारतन्त्र्यान् न पृथक् सिद्धिरिति[*]। [O]तत्संस्थानाधारात्मकं तद् द्रव्यं संस्थानं[*] वा तदाधेयात्मकं प्रकृत्या [3]किं कुलालमपेक्षन्त इति चेत्, न, ततः परस्परसम्बन्धयोग्यताप्रतिलम्भात्। अन्यथा प्रागपि मृत्पिण्डस्य संस्थानविशेषसम्बन्ध[4]योग्यत्वे वस्तुधर्मतयैव संस्थानविशेषसम्बन्ध[*]प्रसङ्गः। [P]एवं तर्हि सा योग्यता मृद्द्रव्यस्य कुलालात्[*]। न चानयोः स्वभावभेदः, [5]भेदे वा[*] पूर्ववत् प्रसङ्गादिति। अस्ति तावत् किञ्चिदेकस्वभावत्वे ऽप्यनेकप्रत्ययोपहितस्वभावविशेषमिति न निर्ब- ms 9a न्धो[*Q] मृत्संस्थानयोरेकस्व[1]भावत्वसाधने[k] ॥ b.122141

[h-h] Ci Utp 44,7–8 [i-i] HBṬ 109,21–22 [j-j] Ci Utp 45,5–7 [k-k] Ci' PVṬ$_t$ Je,169b6–170a3

[N] ‹vaiśeṣikaḥ prāha› gl. ms [O] ‹paro bauddhamatam āśāṅkyāha› gl. ms [P] ‹(bauddhaḥ prāha)› gl. ms [Q] ‹asmākaṃ› gl. ms

---

[1] ca n.e. T [3] dbyibs daṅ 'ji ba'i ṅo bo dag tu T for saṃsthānamṛtsvabhāvaviśeṣābhyām [5] mṛd° n.e. T » bhinna‹ḥ› svabhāva‹ḥ› ms [6] °piṇḍa° n.e. T » tat° n.e. T [8] byed do T for siddhir iti [8–9] dbyibs de T for saṃsthānam [12] 'brel ba'i khyad par du T for °sambandha° » rdza mkhan las 'gyur bas T for kulālāt [13] tha dad pa yin na ni T for bhede vā [14–15] mi 'dod do T for na nirbandhaḥ

[ε] mṛtsaṃsthāna° Utp for saṃsthānamṛtsvabhāva° [ζ] bhinnasvabhāvaḥ Utp for bhinnaḥ svabhāvaḥ [η] api ca om. Utp

(b.12214) [l]तेनसहकारिणः प्रत्यया नैकोपयोगविषयाः कार्यस्यैकस्वभावत्वे ऽपि वस्तुत इति यथेह कारणभेदो भिन्न[*]विशेषोपयोगा[2]न् नैककार्यः, तथा चक्षुरादिभ्यो [*]विज्ञानोत्पत्तावुन्नेयः। [m]तथा हि [n]समनन्तरप्रत्ययाद् विज्ञानाच्[*θ] चक्षुर्विज्ञानस्योपलम्भात्मता, [*]तस्यैवोपलम्भा[3]त्मनः[ι] सतश्[*] चक्षुरिन्द्रियाद् रूपग्रहणयोग्यताप्रतिनियमः, विषयात् तत्तुल्यरूपतेत्यभिन्नत्वे ऽपि वस्तुतः [o]कार्यस्य[κ] कारणानां[*] भिन्नेभ्यः [4]स्वभावेभ्यो भिन्ना एव विशेषा[λo] भवन्तीति[n] न[*μ] कारणभेदे ऽप्यभेदस् [ν]तत्कार्यविशेषस्ये[m]ति[*] त एवैते[ξ] कारणशक्तिभेदा यथास्वं प्रतिवि[5]शिष्टकार्यजनने ऽव्यवधेय[o]शक्तितया प्रत्युपस्थिताः क्षणिकत्वात् सामग्रीकार्यस्य स्वभावस्थित्याश्रय इत्युच्यन्ते[π]। तथा हि तत् तेभ्यः सम[6]स्तेभ्य[ρ] उपलम्भात्मकं रूपग्रहणप्रतिनियतं[σ] विषयरूपं चेति, प्रतिविशिष्ट[τ]स्वभावमेकं[υ] जातमि[l]ति[*] ॥ T 48,25 HBṬ 110,1

[l-l] **Ci'** PVṬ$_t$ Je,170a3–170b1; **Cie** Utp 44,12–45,4 [m-m] **Ci'** AAĀ 972,23–27 (cf. Moriyama 1991: 204) [n-n] **Ci** DAṬ 192,15–18 [o-o] **Cie** AJP II 168,3–4; 174,3–4; 175,7–8

---

2 yul T for °viśeṣa° **3** °bhyo vijñāno° em. (cf. Utp, HBṬ 110,26) : °bhyo pi jñāno° ms » mig gi rnam par śes pa T for vijñāno° **4** vijñānāt n.e. T » tasyaiva n.e. T **5** sataḥ n.e. T (n.e. AAĀ) **6** rgyu'i T for kāraṇānām **7** na n.e. T **8** iti n.e. T

[θ] °pratyayāvijñānāc Utp for °pratyayād vijñānāc [ι] °upalambham ātmanaḥ Utp for °upalambhātmatā tasyaivopalambhātmanaḥ [κ] kāryasya nirvibhaktarūpasya AAĀ for kāryasya [λ] svabhāvā (v.l. viśeṣā) AAĀ for viśeṣā [μ] bhavanti, tena Utp for bhavantīti na [ν] tatkāryasya AAĀ for tatkāryaviśeṣasya [ξ] te ye caite Utp for ta evaite [o] avyābādha° Utp for avyavadheya° [π] ucyate Utp for ucyante [ρ] samastebhya om. Utp [σ] °grahaṇaṃ pratiniyataṃ Utp for grahaṇapratiniyataṃ [τ] viśiṣṭa° Utp for prativiśiṣṭa° [υ] ekam eva Utp for ekam

T 50,15 HBṬ 113,6 ms 9b [R][p]अप्रतिरोधशक्तिकेष्वनन्तरकार्येषु क्षणिकेष्व[1]नाधेयविशेषेषु प्रत्ययेषु परस्परं कः सहकारार्थ इति चेत्, [q]न वै सर्वत्रातिशयोत्पादनं सहक्रिया, किं तर्ह्येकार्थकरणमपि[*] यद्बहूनाम्[q], यथाऽन्त्य[2]स्य कारणकलापस्य। [S]तदेव मुख्यं सहकारिणां सहकारित्वम्, तस्यैवान्त्यस्य कारणत्वात्, तत्र च[*] क्षण एकस्य स्वभावस्याविवेकाद्[T] वि[3]शेषस्य कर्तुमशक्यत्वात्, स्वभावान्तरोत्पत्तिलक्षणत्वाद् विशेषोत्पत्तेः। भावान्तरप्रसवसम्भवे[*] च नान्त्यः स्यात्। ततश् च न साक्षा[4]त्कारणं स्यात्। तस्मान् न कारणस्य सहकारिभ्यो विशेषोत्पत्तिः। [r]ते समर्था एव स्वभावतो ऽन्त्याः प्रत्ययाः सह जायन्ते क्षणिका [5]येषां प्राक्पश्चात्पृथग्भावो नास्ति[r], यतो ऽनन्तरं कार्योत्पत्तिः, तत्रैकार्थक्रियैव सहकारिणां[*] सहकारित्वम्[p]॥ b.12215

T 52,1 [st]समर्थः[*] कुत उत्पन्न इ[6]ति चेत्, स्वकारणेभ्यः[*]॥ b.122151

तान्येनमपरप्रत्ययसन्निधान एव किं जनयन्ति[*], [*]कदाचिदन्यथापि b.1221511

ms 10a स्युः[φ]। ततश् [*]चैको ऽपि क्वचिज् जनयेदिति चेत्, [uv]अपरापर[1]प्रत्यययोगेन[v] प्रतिक्षणं[X] भिन्नशक्तयः सन्तन्वन्तः संस्काराः[*], यद्यपि कुत-

---

p-p **Ci' PVṬ$_t$ Je,170b1–5** q-q cf. HBṬ 127,28–29 r-r cf. HBṬ 124,28–125,2 s-s **Cie** VR 9,15–19 t-t **Ci' PVṬ$_t$ Je,170b5–171a4** u-u cf. HBṬ 89,1–4; 133,26–29 v-v HBṬ 138,18

R ‹(atrāpi paraḥ)› gl. ms S ‹kasmāt› gl. ms T ‹abhedāt› gl. ms

---

3 don gcig byed pas kyaṅ T for ekārthakriyāpi » api n.e. T **5** ca n.e. T **7** 'byuṅ na T for °prasavasambhave **10–11** sahakāriṇām n.e. T **12** nus pa de dag T for samarthaḥ » svakāraṇebhyaḥ em. : svakāraṇebhyus ms **13** rkyen gźan daṅ med pa kho nar ci ste mi skyed de T for aparapratyayasannidhāna eva kiṃ janayanti » de res 'ga' T for kadācit **14** ca n.e. T **15** saṃskārā‹ḥ› ms

---

φ anyathā syāt VR for anyathā syuḥ X pratyabhikṣaṇam VR for pratikṣaṇam

श्चित् साम्यात् सरूपाः प्रतीयन्ते, तथापि भिन्न एवैषां स्वभावः, [w]तेन
किञ्चिदेव कस्यचित् कार[2]णम्[suw] ॥

122151) [xy]तत्र यो ऽव्यवधानादिदेशरूपेन्द्रियादिकलापः, स विज्ञानजनने स- HBṬ 117,15
मर्थो हेतुः[y]। [z]यस् तेषां परस्परोपसर्पणाद्याश्रयः प्रत्ययविशे[3]षः, स
तद्धेतुजनने समर्थः[z]। [a]तेषां च न पूर्वं न पश्चान् न पृथग् भाव इति
समर्थानपि पूर्वापरपृथग्भावभाविनो दोषा नोपलीयन्ते[a]। तेनैषां [4]पर-
स्परोपसर्पणादिहेतुर्यः, स समर्थहेतुरिति तस्य न कदाचिदप्यन्यथा-
भावः। अनेन न्यायेन सर्वत्र हेतुफलभावप्रतिनियम [5]उन्नेयः, प्रतिक्ष-
णमपरापरस्वभावभेदान्वयिनीषु भावशक्तिषु, न स्थिरैकस्वभावेषु भा-
वेषु*, स्वभावान्यथात्वाभावात् समर्थासमर्थस्वभावयोः क्रिया[1]क्रिया- ms 10b
योगात्[t] ॥

1221512 [b*]अन्यसहितः करोति, न केवल इति चेत्, किं केवलस्य [U]कार्यजनने T 52,25 HBṬ 118,22
न समर्थः स्वभावः। समर्थः*। किं न करोति। अकुर्वन् कथं समर्थः[x],
कु[2]विन्दाद[V]यः पटादिकरणे समर्था अपि न सर्वदा कुर्वन्तीति चेत्,
[c]क्रीडनशीलो देवानाम्प्रियः सुखैधितः[c] कृतं कृतं पुनः कारयति। तथा
[3]हि बीजाद्युपन्यासे निर्लोठितमेतत्। तस्मात् *तत्स्वभावस्यान्यथा-
त्वाभावात् तद्धर्मणस् तथाभावो ऽन्त्यावस्थावदनिवार्यः ॥

---

w-w HBṬ 117,14 x-x **Ci** VR 13,6–15 y-y HBṬ 134,19–20 z-z HBṬ 134,27–28
a-a HBṬ 135,10–11 b-b **Ci'** PVṬ$_t$ Je,171a4–7 c-c **Ci'e** Utp 55,9

U ‹sva› gl. ms V ‹tantravāpa› gl. ms

9–10 ‹bhāveṣu› ms **12** anya° n.e. T **13** nus sam mi nus so ‖ T for na samarthaḥ svabhāvaḥ | samarthaḥ | **16** tat° n.e. T

अन्त्यावस्थायां प्राग्[4]समर्थस्य* सामर्थ्योत्पत्तौ *तत्सामर्थ्यस्य b.12215
तत्स्वभावत्वे ऽपूर्वोत्पत्तिरेव सा*। अतत्स्वभावत्वे सो ऽकारक एव,
सामर्थ्याख्यात् पदार्थान्तरात्* कार्योत्पत्तेः[b] ॥

T 54,10 HBṬ 121,8 [5][d]अपि च स तदैव* तावत् *सन्निहितसकलसहकारी कार्यं किं b.12215
करोति। कुर्वन् दृष्टः, तेन करोतीति ब्रूमः। महासामर्थ्यं[Ψ] महाप्रभाव-
ms 11a स्य भवतो* दर्शनं, [W]यदिदं* भावानत[1]त्स्वभावानपि स्वभावमात्रेण
चित्रेषु व्यापारेषु* नियुङ्क्ते*। यदि नाम* कदाचित्* किञ्चित् कथंचिदत्र
भवतो दर्शनविषयम*[X]तिक्रामेत्, हन्त, अप्रसवधर्मकमपेतसन्तानं
[2]स्यादितीयं नश्* चिन्ता चित्तं दुनोति[Y]। न वै[Z] वयमतत्स्वभावानां
*भावानामस्मद्दर्शनात् कार्यक्रियां ब्रूमः। किं तर्हि तत्क्रियाधर्माणः
स्वभाव[3]त एव ते। तान् पश्यन्तो विद्मः – त एते कारका इति।
सत्यम्, इदमप्यस्ति – स्वभावस् तेषां कार्यक्रियाधर्मा। तेन न सम-
स्तप्रत्ययानां *कार्यमकृत्वो[4]पेक्षापत्तिरिति, स किं तेषामक्षेपक्रियाधर्मा
स्वभावस् तदैवान्त्यावस्थायामुत्पन्न आहोस्वित्* प्रागप्यासीत्। आ-
ms 11b सीत्*, अप्रच्युतोत्पन्नस्थिरैक[1]स्वभावानां भावानां* कदाचित् कस्य-

---

[d-d] **Ci'** PVṬ$_t$ Je,171a6–171b5

[W] ‹paramatam āśaṅkāt⁰› gl. ms [X] ‹paṭha iti kvacit pāṭhaḥ› gl. ms (cf. lam la T) [Y] ‹kṣiṇotīti kvacit› gl. ms [Z] ‹vilakṣya prāha› gl. ms

---

1 nus pa med pa las T for asamarthasya » tat° n.e. T **2** sā n.e. T **3** dṅos po las T for padārthāntarāt **4** de ñid T for sa tadaiva » ‹sannihita›sakala° ms **5–6** ‹mahāprabhāvasya bhavato› ms **6** yad idam n.e. T **7** vyāpāre<ṣu> em. (cf. HBṬ 121,25; bya ba sna tshogs pa rnams la T) : vyāpāre ms » sbyor ba ni T for niyuṅkte » 'das na T for yadi nāma ... atikrāmet » ‹kadācit› ms; brgya źig la T for kadācit **8** mthoṅ ba'i lam T for darśanaviṣayam **9** naḥ n.e. T **10** bhāvānām n.e. T **13** kāryam n.e. T **14** ahosvit em. : ahośvit ms **14–15** āsīt n.e. T **15** bhāvānām n.e. T

[Ψ] aho mahāsāmarthyam HBṬ 121,20

चित् स्वभावस्याभावविरोधात्। तत् किमिदानीं [e]माता च वन्ध्या च[e],
को वास्य भाषितस्यार्थः – अक्षेपक्रियास्वभावो[*] [2]न करोति च[d] ॥

1221523 [fg]सहितस् तत्स्वभावो न केवल[f] इति चेत्, अन्यस् तर्हि केवलः[*], T 56,3 HBṬ 123,10
अन्यः [a1]सहितः, स्वभावभेदलक्षणत्वाद् भावभेदस्य। [hi]न हि स[*] सा- msS a1
हित्ये[3]ऽपि[i] पररूपेण कर्ता। स्वरूपं चास्य प्रागपि[h] तदेवेति कथं क-
दाचित् [A]क्रियाविरामः। यस्यापि क्षणिको भावः, तस्यापि[*] किं न के-
वलः करो[4]ति। करोत्येव यदि केवलः[*] स्यात्। किं न भवति। क्षणि-
कत्वात्, उक्तमत्र[*] यादृशस्य क्रिया। स कथमेक[*]क्षणभाव्यन्यथा[*]
स्यात्। [j]यश् च[*] भवति, स [5]एव न भवतीति नायं प्रसङ्गः[j], कारका-
कारकयोः स्वभावतद्धेत्वोर्विरोधात्॥

1221524 [k]यो ऽपि मन्यते – [l]अक्षेपक्रियाधर्मैव स तस्य स्वभावः[l], न स[*] सा- T 56,13 HBṬ 125,18
हित्यम[1]पेक्षते, [m]कार्यं तु प्रत्ययान्तरापेक्षमि[m]ति सहितेभ्य एव जायते, ms 12a
न केवलेभ्य इति, तस्यापि[*] – कथं स[ω] केवलो ऽपि[*] करोत्येव कार्यं च
तस्मान् नोत्पद्यत इ[2]ति तदवस्थो[*] विरोधः। न केवलः करोत्येवेति

[e-e] HBṬ 127,7 [f-f] HBṬĀ 359,23 [g-g] **Ci'** PVṬ$_t$ Je,171b5–172a8 [h-h] **Cie** VR 8,2–3 [i-i] HBṬ 124,15 [j-j] HBṬ 125,15 [k-k] **Ci'** Utp 140,9–14 [l-l] HBṬ 126,4–5 [m-m] HBṬ 126,29

[A] ‹kārya› gl. ms

---

2 mi sdod par skyed pa'i chos kyi ṅo bo ñid kyaṅ yin la T for akṣepakriyāsvabhāvaḥ **3** 'ba' źig kyaṅ T for kevalaḥ **4** sa n.e. T **6** tasyāpi : tasya msSa2; de'i ltar na yaṅ T for tasyāpi **7** kevalaḥ n.e. T **8** atra n.e. T » eka° n.e. T » anyathā em. : ānyathā ms **9** ca n.e. T **11** ‹sa› ms **13** de'i ltar na yaṅ T for tasyāpi » api om. msSa5 **14** gnas skabs de ni T for tadavasthaḥ

[ω] sa bhāvaḥ Utp for sa

चेत्, कथमिदानीम*क्षेपक्रियास्वभावः*। नन्वेतदेव परिदीपितं भवति msS b1 – करो[3]त्येवेति। कार्यं चायं केवलो ऽपि समर्थः सन् प[b1]रमपेक्षमाणं कथमुपेक्षेत। परमनादृत्यैतत्* प्रसह्य कुर्यात्*। एवं *ह्यनेनात्मनः*[α] सामर्थ्यमपि[β] दर्शितं भवति। का[4]र्ये*[γ] परमपेक्षत इति ततः* केवलाद्-नुत्पत्तिरुक्ता भवति। स[δ] केवलो ऽपि समर्थस्वभाव इति तत उत्पत्ति-रिति*[ε], एते *चैकत्र कथं स्याताम्। तदय[5]मीर्ष्याशल्यवितुद्यमानमर्मा* विक्लवं विक्रोशतीत्युपेक्षामर्हति[k]॥

T 58,5 HBṬ 127,19 तस्मादिदमे*का*र्थक्रियालक्षणं सहकारित्वं क्षणिकानामेव भावानां* (b.122152 सम्भवति, न स[6]म्भवत्पृथग्भावानाम*क्षणिकानाम्, पृथक्करण*सम्भवेन सहकारित्वनियमायोगात्[g]॥

ms 12b [n]यत्र तु सन्तानोपकारेण भावाः प्रत्ययतां प्रतिपद्यन्ते[1] यथा तण्डुल*- b.122153 बीजादिभ्य ओदनाङ्कुरादिजन्मनि दहनोदकपृथिव्यादयः, तत्र विशेषो-त्पादनं प्रत्ययानां सहक्रिया सन्तानाश्रयेणोच्यते, न द्रव्याश्र[2]येण, क्ष-णिके द्रव्ये विशेषानुपपत्तेः*। न हि त*ण्डुला*दीनां दहनोदकादिभ्यः*

[n-n] **Ci'** PVṬ$_t$ Je,172a8–172b6

---

1 i{ā}dānīm ms » a[kṣe]pakriyāsvabhāvaḥ msSa6 (Utp; mi sdod par skyed pa'i ṅo bo ñid T) : akṣepakriyādharmā svabhāvaḥ ms **3** ‹param anādṛtyaitat prasahya ku[r]yāt |› ms » anādṛtyaitat : an{n}ādyatyenat msSb1 » hi n.e. T » °ātmanaḥ msSb1 (Utp) : sātmanaḥ ms **4** ‹tataḥ› ms **5–6** skye bar smras pa yin na T for utpattir iti **6** ca n.e. T » °marmā em. (cf. Utp 140,14; HBṬ 127,12) : °marmma ms **8** idam n.e. T » °artha° n.e. T » bhāvānāṃ em. (msSb4) : bhavānāṃ ms **9** yod pa rnams kyi T for °bhāvānām » skyed par T for °karaṇa° **11** 'bras thug po che T for taṇḍula° **14** 'byuṅ ba med pa'i phyir ro T for °anupapatteḥ » end of msSb » 'bras thug po che T for taṇḍula° » me la sogs pa la T for dahanodakādibhyaḥ

[α] hi om. Utp [β] api om. Utp [γ] kārye na Utp for kāryaṃ [δ] sa om. Utp [ε] iti om. Utp

क्रमेण स्वभावातिशयानुत्पत्तावोदनाद्यभिनिर्वृत्तिर[*]स्ती[3]न्द्रियस्य वा
प्रभास्वरादपवरकं[*] प्रविष्टस्य[*] स्वोपकारिभ्यः [*]स्वसन्तानविशेषानुत्प-
त्तावर्थप्रतिपत्तिजननम्॥

[o]अक्षेप[B]कारिषु पुनरिन्द्रि[4]यादिषु न परस्परतो विशेषोत्पत्तिः[o]। तत्र T 58,21 HBṬ 129,8
[p]यथास्वं प्रत्ययैः परस्परोपसर्पणाद्याश्रयैर्ये[*] योग्यदेशाद्यवस्था जा-
ताः, ते सह स्वभाव[5]निष्पत्त्या ज्ञानहेतुतां[*] प्रतिपद्यन्त[p] इत्येकार्थक्रि-
यैव सहकारित्वम्। यत्र तु विशेषोत्पादनेन सहकारिणां प्रत्ययत्वम्,
तत्र हेतुसन्तानस्य प्रत्यया[1][*]न्तरापेक्षेति ततः स्वभावान्तरप्रतिलम्भ ms 13a
उच्यते। [q]तत्र स्वरसतः पूर्वक्षणनिवृत्तौ हेतुप्रत्ययानां तेभ्य एव वि-
शिष्टक्षणविशेषोत्पत्तिः[*q], क्रमेणातिशयवतो[2]ऽन्त्यात् कारणकलापात्
कार्योत्पत्तिः[*n]॥

[C r]सहकारिणः समुत्पन्नविशेषात् कारणात् कार्योत्पत्तौ विशेषस्यैवो- T 60,1 HBṬ 130,21
त्पत्तिर्न स्यात्[*]। [s]अविशिष्टाद् विशेषो[3]त्पत्तौ कार्यस्यापि स्यात्[s]। त-
तश्[*] च परस्परतो विशेषोत्पादानपेक्षिणः सहकारिणः कार्यं कुर्युः।
तेनाक्षणिकानामपि सहकार्यनपे[4]क्षिणां[*] कारणता स्यात्। न चापेक्ष्ये-
भ्यः स्वभावातिशयोत्पत्तिः। [t]अथ विशेषोत्पत्तावपि सहकारिणा कृ-

---

o-o cf. HBṬ 129,8–10 p-p **Ci** HBṬ 134,29–135,2 q-q **Cie** HBṬ 134,4 r-r **Ci'** PVṬ$_t$ Je,172b6–173b3 s-s **Ci** HBṬ 132,1–2 t-t cf. HBṬ 137,2–4

B ‹avilambita› gl. ms C ‹paraḥ prāha› gl. ms

---

1 'grub pa T for abhinirvṛttir **2** apavarakaṃ em. (cf. HBṬ 128,21) : avavarakaṃ ms » praviṣṭasya em. (cf. HBṬ 128,21) : pravṛṣṭasya ms » sva° n.e. T **5** ye n.e. T **6** śes pa'i rkyen ñid du T for jñanahetutām **8** antara n.e. T **9–10** skad cig ma khyad par can 'byuṅ ba'i phyir T for viśiṣṭakṣaṇaviśeṣotpattiḥ **11** 'bras bu'i bar du 'byuṅ T for kāryotpattiḥ **13** mi ruṅ T for na syāt **13–14** tataḥ n.e. T **15** sahakārya<na>pekṣiṇāṃ em. (lhan cig byed pa la mi ltos pa rnams T) : sahakāryapekṣiṇāṃ ms

तविशेष एवोपतिष्ठेत, अनवस्थै[5]वं स्यात्[t]। न च सहकारिणो नित्यं परस्परस्य कार्योत्पादानुगुणविशेषोत्पादनयोग्यावस्थाः, येन नित्यानु-[ms 13b]षक्त एवैषां परस्परकृतो विशेषः स्यात्, [1]तदुपायापाययोः कार्यव्यक्तिविरामदर्शनात्। तेनाद्यो विशेषः सहकारिभ्यो निरुपकारस्य नोत्पद्येतेति[*] ॥

[HBṬ 132,20] [D] [u]नास्माकं पुनः पुनर्वचने[u] कश्चिदुद्वेगः। यद्ये[2]वमपि लोकस्य न्यायप्रतिपत्तिः स्यात्, पुनरपि ब्रूमः[*]। न विशेषोत्पादनादेव सहकारिणां[*] सहकारित्वम्, येन तदभावाद् विशेषोत्पत्तावसहकारिणः स्युः, [3]किं तर्ह्येकार्थक्रियापि[*]। सापि न भवेन् निर्विशेषाणां परस्परतः, भावे वा तदवस्थायामिव पृथगपि स्यात्। तथा च तद्विशेषभावि कार्यमपि [4]के-[T 60,26]वलात् स्यादिति चेत्, सर्वमुक्तम्[*] – प्रतिक्षणमपरापरैः प्रत्ययैर्यथा भावसन्ताने विशेषोत्पत्तिः, योग्यदेशताद्यवस्थाभेदाः कार्यका[5]रिणः, तेषां च यत उत्पत्तिः, प्रत्येकं सामर्थ्ये ऽपि यथा केवलानामक्रिया कर्तृविशेषपृथग्भावाभावात्, कार्यद्वैविध्यं च – सहकारिजनितविशेष-[ms 14a]प[1]रम्परोत्पत्तिधर्मकमन्यच् च, अङ्कुरादिवदक्षेपकारीन्द्रियविज्ञानादिवच्[*] च, कार्यकारणस्वभावभेदादिति। तत्र सहकारिभ्यः सन्तानोपकारापेक्ष[2][*]कारणकार्यजन्मन्याद्यः सहकारिविशेषो न[*] सहकारिकृतविशेषजन्मा ऽनन्तरकार्यवत्। ततः प्रभृति ये विशेषास् ते तज्जन्मा-

---

[u-u] Ci HBṬ 134,2

[D] ‹bauddhaḥ prāha› gl. ms

---

5 mi ’thad do źe na T for notpadyeteti **7** ’gyur ba ltar na da duṅ yaṅ smra bar bya’o T for syāt, punar api brūmaḥ » ‹sahakāriṇāṃ |› ms **9** don gcig byed pas kyaṅ T for ekārthakriyāpi **11** cf. sarvam uktam HBṬ 133,16 (T 62,6) **15–16** °vijñānā‹di›vac ms; ādi n.e. T **17** ’bras bu’i rgyu T for kāraṇakārya° » ‹sahakāriviśeṣaḥ | na› ms

नस् तत्प्रकृतिकत्वात्*, तस्य तेषां चेति* नानव[3]स्था। तथा* यद्यक्षणिको ऽपि भावो ऽनाहितातिशयः *सहकारिणाद्यविशेषहेतुवत्* कार्यं कुर्वीत, करोतु*। स पुनरस्य स्वभावो ऽक्षेपकर्तृधर्मा चेत्, पृथ[4]ग्भावसम्भवात्, केवलो ऽपि तथा स्यादित्युक्तम्। अतत्स्वभावस् तु तदाप्यकारक एव॥

(b.122) तस्मान्[r] नाक्षणिकेषु हेतुष्वेकार्थक्रियया* कस्यचित् सहकारित्व[5]नि- (T 62,20 HBṬ 137,20) यमो नापि सन्तानोपकारेणेति न तस्य कश्चित् सहकारी ततः केवलो ऽपि कुर्यादिति*, प्रायस्तु सङ्घातस्थायी भावसन्तानः सहकारिप्रत्ययो[6]पजनितविशेषः स्वकार्यं कुर्वन् दृष्टो बीजादिवदिति*। स्थिरहेतुवादिनः* प्रत्ययान्तरापेक्षा* व्यक्तं कारकस्वभावान्तरोत्पत्तिरिति। नाकार्यस्यापेक्षेत्युच्यते*,[1] कारकस्वभावस्य प्रागपि भावे ऽक्रियाऽयोगात्*॥ (ms 14b)

b.123 तस्माद्[v] यो यदात्मा स *स्वसत्तामात्रेण तादृशो भवति। न च भूत्वा (T 64,1 HBṬ 138,24) पुनस् तद्भावे[ζ] ऽपरा[η]भिसंस्कारमपेक्षत इति*। स्वभा[2]वतो ऽस्थितिधर्मणो भावस्य न किञ्चिन् नाशकारणैः[v]। स्थितिधर्मणो ऽपि केनचित् स्वभावान्यथाभावस्य कर्तुमशक्यत्वात् किं नाशकारणैः। अन्यथात्वप्र[3]तिपत्तौ वा तत्स्वभाव एव न स्यादिति पूर्वो विकल्पस् तत्र चोक्तम्। [w]यश्

---

v-v Ci Utp 76,13–14 w-w HBṬ 140,20

---

1 tatprakṛti‹ka›tvāt ms » iti n.e. T » tathā n.e. T **2** sahakāriṇa° n.e. T » viśeṣa‹hetu›vat ms **3** bskyed la ni rag ste T for karotu **6** °kriyayā em. (HBṬ 137,19) : °kriyā ms **8** iti n.e. T **9** iti n.e. T » rgyu rtag par smra ba'i ltar na T for sthirahetuvādinaḥ **10** ‹pratyayāntarā›pekṣā ms; °antara° n.e. T; ltos pa yin na T for °apekṣā **10–11** 'bras bu la ltos pa źes bya'o T for nākāryasyāpekṣety ucyate **11** mi ruṅ ṅo T for ayogāt **12** sva° n.e. T **13** iti n.e. T

ζ na bhūtvā tadbhāve Utp for na ca bhūtvā punar tadbhāve η parā° Utp for 'parā°

च परस्मादन्यथाभावः सो ऽपरः स्वभावः[W], यश् चापरः स कथं तस्य* स्वभावभेदलक्षणत्वाद् भावभेदस्य। त[4]था च पूर्वको भावो ऽप्रच्युतिधर्मे स्थित इति न तस्यान्यथाभावः॥

T 64,14 HBṬ 140,3 [E]एतेन कठिनादीनां ताम्रादीनामग्न्यादिभ्यो *द्रवत्वादिस्वभावान्तरोत्पत्तिः* प्रत्यु[5]क्ता। तत्रापि पूर्वकस्य स्वरसनिरोधित्वाद् *विनाशे सत्यग्न्यादेरुपादानाच् चापर एव *द्रवस्वभाव उत्पन्न इति*॥

T 64,19 HBṬ 140,27 [F]स स्वयं स्थितिधर्मैव, विनाशहेत्व[6]सम्भवे ऽवस्थानात्। तस्य पर- b.1231 स्माद् विनाशः, न च विनाशो नामापरः स्वभावः, भावप्रच्युतिरेव वि- ms 15a नाश इति। [G]नेदमुत्तरं विकल्पद्वयमतिक्रामति। किं नित्यो भावः [1]स्वभावत *आहोस्विदनित्य इति विकल्पे* प्राङ् नित्यो भूत्वा पश्चादनित्यो भवतीति* ब्रुवाणो भावद्वयं* नित्यानित्यस्वभावभेदम्, पूर्वकस्य नित्याभिमतस्य स्वयं ना[2]शमनाशं च सर्वदा प्राहेत्यसमर्थः पूर्वस्मिन् पक्षे* विनाशहेतुः। [H]न प्राङ् नित्यो भूत्वा पश्चादनित्यो भवति, किं तर्हि पश्चादपि नित्य एव, एकस्वभावत्वा[3]त्। स तर्हि भावः स्वभावेन विनाशमनाविशन् कथं नष्टो नाम, तत्स्वभावविनाशयोः परस्परपरिहाररूपत्वात्*॥

[E] ‹pratyākhyati› gl. ms [F] ‹paraḥ prāha› gl. ms [G] ‹bauddhaḥ prāha› gl. ms [H] ‹nṛyonisa? evāha› gl. ms

---

1–2 ‹yaś cāparaḥ sa kathaṃ tasya› ms **4** sñi ba T for dravatva° **4–5** gźan du ’gyur ba T for °antarotpattiḥ **5–6** źig na T for vināśe sati **6** sñi ba la sogs pa’i T for drava° » iti n.e. T **10** āhosvid em. : āhośvid ms » brtag par bya ba la T for vikalpe **11** bhavatīti em. : bhavātīti ms » daṅ add. T **13** ‹pakṣe› ms; pakṣe n.e. T **15–16** phan tshun gyi ṅo bo can ma yin pa ñid kyi phyir T for parasparaparihārarūpatvāt (cf. aparasparārūpatvāt parasparaparihārarūpatvāt HBṬ 143,10)

(b.1) तस्मात् सत्यस्य विनाशे[*] विनाश[4]स्वभावेनैवा[*]नेन भवितव्यम्। तथापि व्यर्थो विनाशहेतुरित्युक्तम्, तेन [x]स्वभावतो नश्वरेऽनश्वरे[θ] वा भावे न विनाशहेतोरुपयोगः॥ T 66,3 HBṬ 143,12

(b.) तस्माद्[y]विना[5]शे ऽनपेक्षो[*] भावस् तद्भावनियत[y]इति[*] यः सन् स विनाशी[x], नश्वरतानिवृत्तौ च सत्त्वनिवृत्तिरिति, अन्वयव्यतिरेकसिद्धिः॥ HBṬ 143,26

b.2 स्वभावतो नश्वरत्वे ऽपि [z]कश्चिदत[6]त्स्वभावो ऽपि स्यात्[z], न हि सर्वः सर्वस्य स्वभाव इति नान्वयव्यतिरेकसिद्धिरिति चेत्, न, अक्षणिकत्वे ऽवस्तुत्वप्रसङ्गात्। [ab]शक्तिर्हि भावलक्षणं [b]सर्वशक्तिविरहो ऽभावल[1]क्षणम्[a]। न चाक्षणिकस्य क्वचिच् छक्तिः[*], क्रमयौगपद्याभ्यामर्थ- ms 15b क्रियाविरोधात्। तस्मात् – यत् सत् तत् क्षणिकमेवेति व्याप्तिसिद्धिः॥ T 66,10 HBṬ 144,28

4.20 [c]अर्थान्तरे गम्ये कार्यहेतुर[2]व्यभिचारात्[c]॥ T 66,20

4.21 [d]कार्यकारणभावेन गमकत्वे लिङ्गस्य [e]सर्वथा गम्यगमकभावः, सर्वथा जन्यजनकभावादिति चेत्, न, तदभावे भवतस् तदुत्पत्तिनि[3]यमाभावात्। [f]तस्मात् [g]कार्यं स्वभावैर्यावद्भिरविनाभावि कारणे[ı][g] तेषां हेतुस्[f] तत्कार्यत्वनियमात्, तैरेव च[*] धर्मैर्ये तैर्विना न भवन्ति। अंशेन HBṬ 150,14

---

x-x **Ci** Utp 74,13–14 y-y cf. TBV 323,25–26 z-z HBṬ 145,14 a-a cf. PVin 2.79,3–4; **Ci** Utp 9,9–10; BCAP 195,19–20; NBhū 510,10–11 b-b **Ci** Utp 5,13 c-c **Ce'e** PVin 2.84,2 d-d cf. PVin 2.84,8–85,3 e-e **Ce'e** PVSV 3,10–19 f-f **Ci** Utp 17,12–13 g-g **Ce'** PV 1.2ab

---

1 'jig pa yod pa daṅ T for sati asya vināśe » eva n.e. T **4** ltos pa med pas T for anapekṣaḥ » iti n.e. T **9** 'ga' yaṅ gaṅ du nus pa T for kvacic chaktiḥ **15** ca n.e. T

θ anaśvare naśvare Utp for naśvare 'naśvare ı kāraṇam Utp for kāraṇe

जन्यजन$_{4}$कत्वप्रसङ्ग इति चेत्, न, तज्जन्यविशेषग्रहणे ऽभिमतत्वात्, लिङ्गविशेषोपाधीनां च सामान्यानाम्। अविशिष्टसामान्यविवक्षायां व्यभिचा$_{5}$रान् नेष्यते[de] ॥

T 68,3 HBṬ 153,16 कस्यचित् कदाचित् कुतश्चिद् भावे ऽपि सर्वस् तादृशस् *तथाविध- 4.22
जन्मेति कुतः*। तथा च नान्वयव्यतिरेकाविति चेत्, न, अतद्भाविनः सकृदपि त$_{6}$तो ऽभावात्। परस्परापेक्षया जन्यजनकस्वभावलक्षणे हि* कार्यकारणे। तत्र यदि धूमो ऽग्न्यादिसामग्र्या अन्यतो ऽपि भवेत्, ms 16a न तस्य तज्जन्यः स्वभाव इति स$_{1}$कृदपि ततो* न भवेदर्थान्तरवत्। नापि सामग्री तं जनयेदतज्जननस्वभावत्वात् सामग्र्यन्तरवत्। [h]न च धूमस्य तदतज्जन्यः स्वभावो[h] युक्त एकस्वभावत्वात्। $_{2}$धूमाधूमजननस्वभावाद् भवतो धूमाधूमस्वभावः स्यात्, कार्यस्वभावानां कारणस्वभावकृतत्वादकारणापेक्षणे वा*ऽहेतुकत्वप्र$_{3}$सङ्गात्। तस्मात् सो ऽग्न्यादिसामग्रीविशेषो यो धूमजनकः, स धूमो यो ऽग्न्यादिसामग्रीविशेषजनित इति* कार्यकारणयोरेवं *स्वभावनियमा$_{4}$न् न विजातीयादुत्पत्तिः। तन् न दृष्टं* कार्यं कारणं व्यभिचरति। तेन सिद्धे कार्यकारणभावे कार्यस्य कारणेन व्याप्तिः सिद्धा भवति॥

T 68,27 HBṬ 160,16 [i]ननु विजातीयाद्$_{5}$पि किञ्चिद् भवद् दृष्टं तद् यथा गोमयादेः[l] शालू- 4.221
कादिः[i]। [j]न विजातीयादुत्पत्तिः[j]। तथाविधमेव हि* कारणं* तादृशाम्

[h-h] HBṬ 165,25–26 [i-i] cf. PVSV 23,22–23 [j-j] HBṬ 160,13

---

[l] ‹ādiśabdāt sūryamaṇicandrakāntyādeḥ |› gl. ms

---

4 de las T for tathāvidha° **5** go ga las T for kutaḥ **7** hi n.e. T **8** tataḥ n.e. T **12** yaṅ T for vā **14** iti n.e. T » ‹svabhāva› ms **15** ‹ta[n na dṛṣṭaṃ]› ms; dṛṣṭaṃ n.e. T; cf. iti na kāryaṃ dṛṣṭaṃ kāraṇaṃ vyabhicarati HB 30,11 **18** hi n.e. T » kāraṇaṃ n.e. T

आदिनिमित्तमिति न कारणभेदः। प्रबन्ध[6]वृत्तौ तु शराद् भावः। अस्ति च गोमयेतरजन्मनोः स्वभावभेदो रूपाभेदे ऽपि, न ह्याकारसाम्यमेव भावानां तत्त्वे निबन्धनम्, अभिन्नाकाराणामपि के[1] [ms 16b] षाञ्चिदन्यतो विशेषाज् जातिभेददर्शनात्। अन्यथा हि [k]विलक्षणाया अपि सामग्र्या अविलक्षणस्योत्पत्तौ[κ] न कारणभेदाभेदाभ्यां कार्यभेदाभेदावित्य[l]हे[2]तुकौ विश्वस्य भेदाभेदौ स्याताम्। तथा हि न[*] भेदाद् [*]भेद इत्यभेदाद[λ]पि नाभेदः, तद्व्यतिरिक्तश् च न कश्चिद् भावस्वभाव इत्य[m]-हेतुकत्वाद् भावानां नित्यं स[3]त्त्वमसत्त्वं वा स्यात्[lm], अपेक्ष्याभावात्[μ]। [n]अपेक्षया हि भावाः कादाचित्का[v] भवन्ति[n] व्यवस्थावांश् च साध्येषु साधननियोगो न स्यात्, कारणशक्तिप्रति[4]नियमे[ξ] हि किञ्चिदेव कस्यचित् साधनायोपादीयेत नापरम्, तस्यैव तत्र शक्तेरन्यस्य चाशक्तेः, तयोस्[*]तज्जननेतरस्वभावत्वेन भेदात्। त[5]ज्जननस्वभावविलक्षणादपि तस्योत्पत्तौ न तज्जननशक्तिप्रतिनियम इति यत् किञ्चिद् यतः[*] कुतश्चित्[o] स्यात्, तज्जननशक्तिसाम्ये तु तदे[6]वे[o]ति न कार्यं दृष्टं[π] कारणं व्यभिचरति[*][ko]॥

[k-k] **Cie** Utp 4,3–8 [l-l] cf. AAĀ 970,4–5 [m-m] cf. PV 1.35ab (= PV 2.179cd; PVin 2.58ab) [n-n] **Ce'** PVSV 22,24 [o-o] **Ce'e** PVSV 23,26–27

---

6 na n.e. T **6–7** bheda iti n.e. T **12** tat° n.e. T **13** yata{ś ca}ḥ ms
14–15 'bras bu rgyu 'khrul pa ma mthoṅ ṅo T for na kāryaṃ dṛṣṭaṃ kāraṇam vyabhicarati

---

[κ] avilakṣaṇakāryotpattau Utp for avilakṣaṇasyotpattau [λ] bhedād Utp for abhedād [μ] apekṣyābhāvāt om. Utp [v] kadācit sattvā Utp for kādācitkā [ξ] °pratiniyoge Utp for °pratiniyame [o] yataḥ kutaścit om. Utp [π] kāryadṛṣṭaṃ Utp for kāryaṃ dṛṣṭaṃ

T 70,26 उपलब्धिलक्षणप्राप्तस्या*नुपलब्धिर् अभावहेतुर् अभावव्यवहारहे- 4.30
तुर्वा॥

HBṬ 169,23 ms 17a अत्रोपलब्धेरुपलभमानधर्मत्वे [1]तज्ज्ञानमुपलब्धिः। [pq]तस्मादन्योप- c.111
लब्धिरनुपलब्धिः, [r]विवक्षितोपलब्धेरन्यत्वात्, *अभक्ष्यास्पर्शनीयवत्[q]
पर्युदासवृत्त्या[pr]। उपलभ्यमानधर्मत्वे विषयस्वभाव उपलब्धिः [2]स्ववि- c.112
षयविज्ञानजननयोग्यतालक्षणः, योग्यताया भावरूपत्वात्। तस्माद-
न्य उपलम्भजननयोग्य एव स्वभावो ऽनुपलब्धिः पूर्ववत्*।

यत्र यस्मिन्नुपलभ्यमाने [3]नियमेन यदुपलब्धिर्भवति योग्यताया अ- c.113
विशेषात्, स तत्संसृष्टः, एकज्ञानसंसर्गात्। [s]तयोः सतोर्नैकरूपनिय-
ता प्रतिपत्तिः, असम्भवात्[s]। तस्मादविशि[4]ष्टयोग्यतारूपयोरे[t]क*ज्ञा-
नसंसर्गिणोः[p] परस्परापेक्षमेवान्यत्वमि[t]हेष्टम्। स केवलस् तदपेक्षया
तस्मादन्यः*। तज्ज्ञानं तत्स्वभावो वा *ज्ञातृज्ञेयधर्मल[5]क्षणा ऽनुपल-
ब्धिः। सा ऽभावमभावव्यवहारं वा प्रतियोगिनः साधयति॥

---

p-p **Ci'e** AR 1,5–6 q-q **Ce'e** PVV 285,15–16 r-r HBṬ 172,4 s-s HBṬ 192,22–23; 194,24; **Ci'** SAC 9,3–4; **Ci'e** NBṬ 101,14–15; AR 2,14–15; 10,5 t-t **Ci** TSP² 586,8–9

---

1 rig byar gyur pa T for °lakṣaṇaprāptasya **4** abhakṣyā° (bzar mi ruṅ ba T; HBṬ) : abhakṣā° ms **6–7** de las gźan pa'i dmigs par ruṅ ba kho na ñid mi dmigs pa ste | sṅa ba bźin no || T for tasmād anya ... pūrvavat **10** eka° n.e. T **12** gźan yin pas T for anyaḥ » de śes par byed pa T for jñātṛ°

---

p °saṃsargiṇaḥ TSP (v.l.°saṃsargiṇo 'para°) for saṃsargiṇoḥ

c.21 कथमन्यभावस् तदभावो येनान्यभाव*रूपानुपलब्ध्या ऽभावव्यवहारः सा[6]ध्यते। उक्तम[u]त्र यथा पर्युदासवृत्त्या ऽपेक्षातो ऽभावानुपलब्धी, न प्रतिषेधमात्रमिहानुपलब्धिः*, तस्य साधनासिद्धेरभावव्यवहारासिद्धिप्रसङ्गात्। तस्यासंसृष्ट[7]रूपस्य भावसिद्धिरेवापरस्याभावसिद्धिरित्यन्यभावो ऽपि तदभाव इति व्यपदिश्यते॥ T 72,15 HBṬ 175,3

c.22 अन्यभावलक्षणो ऽभावः स्वयं प्रमाणेन सिद्धस्* तदभावव्यव[1]हारं साधयेत्, तत्सि[J]द्धिसिद्धो वा तदभाव इति न कश्चिद् विशेषो येनानुपलब्ध्या ऽभावव्यवहारसिद्धिविरोधः स्यात्। [v]स एवान्यभावस् तद्विषया चोपलब्धिस्* *त[2]दभावस्य किं न साधनम्[v], किं पुनरन्यभावसिद्धिरेव तदभावसिद्धिरिति, [K][w]अपृथक्सिद्धेः[w] [x]सम्बन्धाभावाच् च[x] ॥ HBṬ 177,28 ms 17b

---

[u] cf. HB § c.111 [v-v] HBṬ 200,17–18, 20–21 [w-w] HBṬ 200,28 [x-x] HBṬ 185,3

[J] ‹paraḥ prāha |› gl. ms [K] ‹(bauddhaḥ prāha)› gl. ms

---

1 dṅos po med pa'i ṅo bo T for anyabhāva° **3** mi dmigs pa yin par T for na pratiṣedhamātram ihānupalabdhiḥ **6** siddha{si}s ms **9** śes pa T for upalabdhiḥ » tat° n.e. T

T 74,5 c.221 अन्यभावस् तावन् न साधनम्॥

HBṬ 178,28 c.2211 [y]यत्सिद्धौ य[3]स्य न सिद्धिः, तत् तस्य लिङ्गं भवति[y] धूमाग्निवत्। अन्यभावसिद्धयैव तदभावः सिध्यति, तस्य तदन्यासंसृष्टरूपस्य केवलस्य* *तत्त्वव्यवस्थापकादेव प्रमाणा[4]दन्यव्यवच्छेदसिद्धेः॥

HBṬ 180,17 T 74,11 c.2212 सम्बन्धाभावाच् च। तच् च तस्य लिङ्गं भवति* येन यस्य* कश्चित् सम्बन्धो* यथा कृतकत्वानित्यत्वयोरेकार्थसमवायो धूमस्य वा स्वलिङ्गि[5]न्येकार्थसमवाय आधाराधेयभावो वा जन्यजनकभावो वा। नैवं कश्चिद् भावाभावयोः सम्बन्धो येनास्य साधनं स्यात्॥

HBṬ 182,24 c.22121 अस्ति विषयविषयि[6]भावः शब्दार्थवत् सम्बन्ध* इति चेत्, न, शब्दार्थयोस् तत्प्रतिपादनाभिप्राये सति* प्रयोगात् तेन सह कार्यकारण-
ms 18a लक्षणो ऽविनाभावलक्षणो वा सम्बन्धः स्या[1]त्। अयं च प्रकारो ऽत्र न सम्भवति*। कुतो विषयविषयिभावः। सिद्धे हि तयोः[L] साध्यसाधनभावे तन्मुखेन विषयविषयिभावः स्यात्। स एवासति सम्बन्धे न सिध्यति। [2]त[M]दसिद्धौ न विषयविषयिभावः*। अन्यथेतरेतराश्रयमिदं स्यात्॥

T 74,28 c.221211 अन्यभावाच् चाभावसिद्धावसमुदायश् च साध्यः स्यात्। तथा च – घटाभावस् तदन्य[3]भावादिति घटस्य सर्वत्र सर्वदा ऽभावः स्यात्।

---

y-y Ci' PPar II 44,9–10

L ‹śabdārthayoḥ› gl. ms M ‹sambandhāsiddhau› gl. ms

3–4 kevalasya n.e. T **4** tattvavyava° em. : tatve vyava° ms **5–6** daṅ de de'i rtags yin na de daṅ der 'brel pa 'ga' źig tu gyur te T for tac ca ... sambandhaḥ **5** •• •• t[i] | ms » de daṅ der T for yena yasya **9** sgra daṅ don 'brel pa bźin T for śabdārthavat sambhandaḥ **10** de ston na T for tatpratipādanābhiprāye sati **12** sambha‹va›ti ms **14** yaṅ add. T

[N] न, [z] प्रदेशादिधर्मिविशेषणस्याभावस्य साधनादि[z]ति चेत्। स्यादेतत् प्रदेशादेर्धर्मिणो विशेषणभू[4]तो ऽभावः साध्यते न केवलः, तेन नासमुदायसाधनम्। न च लिङ्गलिङ्गिनोरसम्बन्धो ऽन्यभावस्य प्रदेशादिधर्मिसम्बन्धादिति। न, प्रदेशादेरेव तदन्य[5]भावत्वात्। यत्रैव हि प्रदेशादौ* यन् नास्तीत्युच्यते, स एव तदसंसृष्टो ऽन्यभावः। तद्दर्शनादेवास्य घटो नास्तीति भवति। कथं तस्यैव लिङ्गलिङ्गिभावः॥

.2212111 न चा[6]त्र सामान्यविशेषभावविकल्पः सम्भवति, येन सामान्यं हेतुः T 76,10 स्याद् विशेषो धर्मी, *तद्विशेषप्रतिपत्तेरेव तदभावप्रतीतेस् तस्य *चान्यत्रानन्वयात्। प्रतिज्ञार्थैकदे[1]शत्वाच् चालिङ्गत्वम्। [O] न च यत्र प्रदेशमात्रं ms 18b तत्र घटाभावः। तादृशे केवले प्रदेशे ऽभाव एवेति चेत्*, [P] ननु तस्यैव* कैवल्यमिति घटविरह उच्यते। स चेह लिङ्गभूतप्रदेशप्रतिप[2]त्तावेव सिद्धः। कस्येदानीं तल् लिङ्गम्। अन्वयानुगमनं च* निरर्थकम्। तस्मादन्यभावो न साधनमभावस्य॥

c.22122 अस्ति सम्बन्धो विरोधः, ततो ऽन्यभावादभावसिद्धि[3]रिति चेत्, केन HBṬ 187,11 कस्य विरोधः। अन्यभावेन प्रतियोगिनः। किं नु वै प्रतियोगी प्रमातुमिष्टो येन विरोधः सम्बन्धो लिङ्गलिङ्गिनोः। [Q] अभावस् तु प्र[4]तियोगिनो ऽन्यभावेन न विरुध्यते, सहावस्थानात्। तस्मिन् प्रमेये कथं

---

z-z HBṬ 187,8–9

N ‹paraḥ› gl. ms O ‹paraḥ› gl. ms P ‹bauddhaḥ› gl. ms Q ‹bauddhaḥ› gl. ms (better placed before kiṃ nu)

---

5 °ādi n.e. T **8** ‹na› ms (n.e. T; cf. kuto na sambhavati HBṬ 186,1–2) **8–9** cā‹nyatrāna›nvayāt* ms; anyatra n.e. T **10** ’bhāva ‹eveti c[e]› iti cet* ms **11** eva n.e. T **12** anvayānu‹gamanañ ca› ms; smos pa T for anugamanam

विरोधो लिङ्गलिङ्गिनोरित्यसम्बन्ध एव[*]। अत्राप्यसमुदायसाध्यत्वं तदवस्थम्॥

T 76,30 [a]नन्व सति सम्बन्धे तदभावान्यभावयोरन्यभावगत्यापि तदभावगतिर्न स्यात्[a], [b]न वै कुतश्चित् सम्बन्धाद[b]न्यभावस्तदभावस्य गमक इष्यते, अपि त्वन्यभाव एव तदभावः, यथोक्तं प्राक्[c]। तस्यानन्यसंसृष्टरूपस्य केवलस्यैकात्मनि व्यवस्थितस्य तेनात्मना परिच्छेद एवा- ms 19a परस्य व्यवच्छेद इति, [d]तस्य कैवल्यमेवापरवैकल्यमि[d]ति, तदन्यभाव एव तदभावः, [e]तदन्यप्रतिपत्तिरेव च तदप्रतिपत्तिरु[e]च्यते। अन्यथा तत्परिच्छेदेन तदन्याव्यवच्छेदे तत्परिच्छेद एव न स्यात्, तदतद्रूपयोरविवेकादिति[*]। य एष कस्यचिद्दर्शनात् क्वचित् प्राप्तिपरिहारार्थो व्यवहारः, स एव[*] न स्यात्। [fgh]न ह्ययमनलं[*] पश्यन्न[g]प्य[h]नलमेव पश्यति, येन सलिलार्थी तत्र न प्रवर्तेत[f]॥ c.22123

T 78,15
HBṬ 190,4 अनुपलम्भेन सलिलाभावं प्रतिपद्यत इति चेत्, को ऽयमनुपलम्भो नाम। यदि सलिलोपलम्भाभावः, [i]स कथमभावः कस्यचित् प्रतिपत्तिः प्रतिपत्तिहेतुर्वा। तस्यापि कथं प्रतिपत्तिः[i]। कस्यचिदपि तस्य तदन्यस्य वा ऽप्रतिपत्तावपि स्वापमदमूर्छाव्यवधानपराङ्मुखव्यावस्थादिषु किं नाभावप्रतिपत्तिरिति विचारितं प्रमाणविनिश्चये[j]। तस्मादयम[k]नलं c.221231

---

a-a cf. HBṬ 193,23–24 b-b HBṬ 193,24–25 c cf. HB 32,8 or 33,2–3 d-d **Ci'e** AS 114,12 e-e cf. HBṬ 193,25–26 f-f VR 30,3–4 g-g J 218,13 h-h HBṬ 196,8–9 i-i HBṬ 176,16–17; **Ci'e** J 102,14–15; 183,5–6 (= AR 1,4–5); R 28,25–26; 105,8–9; TBh 11,5–6 j cf. PVin 2.58,13–59,11 k-k cf. NM I 77,14; TBV 285,20

---

1 eva n.e. T **10** iti n.e. T **11** ‹eva› ms, n.e. T » a‹yam a›nalaṃ ms; ayam n.e. T

पश्यन्नप्यनलो ऽयं न सलिलमित्यनध्यवस्यन्[l] न तिष्ठेन् न प्रतिष्ठेते[k]ति दुस्तरं व्यसनमापन्नः[l] ॥

c.221232 तत एवैकदर्शनाद्[6] न्याभावप्रतीतिरिति चेत्, कथमेकं पश्यन्नन्यन्[R] नास्तीति प्रतीयात्। तस्यैव[*] केवलस्य दर्शनादिति चेत्, इदमेवास्माभिरुच्यमानं किमत्र भवतः परुषमिवा[1] भाति। तस्मात् तीरादर्शिनेव शकुनिना दूरङ्गत्वापि पुनरागन्तव्यमित्यलमप्रतिष्ठानदिक्प्रतिपत्त्या॥ T 78,27 HBṬ 192,3 ms 19b

c.221233 [S]यद्येकपरिच्छेदादेव अन्यस्य व्यवच्छेदसिद्धिः, अविशेषेणान्यस्य [2]सर्वस्य तत्राभावसिद्धिः स्यात्, न तुल्ययोग्यावस्थस्यैव। उपलब्धिलक्षणप्राप्तस्यानुपलब्धिरभावव्यवहार[*]साधनीति [m]विशेषणं चावाच्यम्[m], अनुपलब्धिलक्षण[3]प्राप्तानामपि तत्र व्यवच्छेदात्। ए[T]कात्मपरिच्छेदात् तस्य तदन्यात्मव्यवच्छेदो भवति, तदात्मनियतप्रतिभासज्ञानात्, न हि तदात्मा तदन्यात्मेति। अव्यवच्छेदे ऽ[4]न्यात्मनः प्रवृत्तिनिवृत्त्योरभाव इति पूर्वः प्रसङ्गः[n]। तं च[*] देशकालस्वभावावस्थानियतं तदात्मनोपलभमाना बुद्धिस् तथात्वप्रच्युतिमस्य व्यवच्छिनत्ति। एवं हि स त[5]या परिच्छिन्नो भवति, यद्यन्यथाभावो व्यवच्छिन्नस् तथात्वं च तस्यैव भवति नान्यस्येत्यन्यथाभूतात् तथाभूतं[*] व्यवच्छि- T 80,6 HBṬ 194,3

[l-l] cf. Vyom II 276,11–12 [m-m] cf. NVTṬ 511,22; ĪPVV II 393,22–23 [n] cf. above § c.2212111

[R] ‹prekṣāvān› gl. ms [S] ‹paraḥ prāha› gl. ms [T] ‹bauddhaḥ› gl. ms

---

4 tasyaiva n.e. T **10** ‹vyavahāra› ms, n.e. T, also om. HBṬ 194,13 **14** ca n.e. T **17** gźan du gyur pa T for anyathābhūtāt* tathābhūtam (tathābhūtād anyathābhūtam HBṬ 196,24)

न्दत्येव तत्परिच्छिनत्तीत्येकप्रमाणवृत्तिः सर्वभा[6]वान् द्वैराश्ये व्यवस्थापयति, तस्यान्वयव्यतिरेकबुद्धिहेतुत्वेनैव साफल्यात्॥

T 80,26 HBṬ 197,12 तद्व्यतिरिक्ताशेषव्यवच्छेदव्याप्तिसाधनादेव प्रकारान्तराभावसिद्धिः, ms 20a तस्य तदन्य[1]तया ऽव्याप्तौ तेन तदर्थाव्यवच्छेदात् पुनर्भावापरिच्छेदप्रसङ्गात्। [o]तस्मात् क्वचित् प्रमाणं प्रवृत्तं [pqr]तत् परिच्छिनत्ति, ततो ऽन्य[σ]द् व्यवच्छिनत्ति[r], तृतीय[τ]प्रकाराभावं च सूचय[2]तीत्ये[q]क[*]प्रमाणव्यापार[p] एषः[o]। तथा हि क्वचित् प्रमाणं प्रवृत्तं तदेव[*] तदन्यस्माद् व्यवच्छिनत्ति, तस्यैव परिच्छेदात्, तदन्यदेव च तस्मात् तदन्यस्य तत्रापरिच्छेदात्। [3]अतस् तदेव प्रमाणं प्रकारान्तराभावं साधयति, तस्मिन् दृश्यमाने ऽदृष्टतदन्यत्वेन सर्वस्य व्यवस्थापनादतदन्यस्यैव च तत्त्वेन व्यवस्थापनात्। [s]एते[4] न क्रमाक्रमादयो[s] ऽन्योन्यव्यवच्छेदरूपा व्याख्याताः॥

T 82,10 तदेवमेकोपलम्भात् तस्य तदन्यात्मनो व्यवच्छेदो भवति, न तद्देशकालयोः सर्वान्यभावव्यवच्छे[5]दः। तस्मादतदात्मा च स्यात् तद्देशकालश् च, रसरूपादिवत्। तस्मात् क्वचित् कदाचित् कस्यचिदभावसिद्धिर्यथोक्तादे[t]वानुपलम्भात् स्यात्॥

T 82,17 HBṬ 200,20 अन्यभावविषया पुनरुप[6]लब्धिस् तदभावस्य साधिकेष्टैव न पुनर्लि- c.222
ङ्गत्वेनैव[*], तत्राप्यभावस्य पृथक् साध्यत्वे सम्बन्धाभावस्य तुल्य-
त्वात्। लिङ्गाविर्भावकाल एव तदभावसिद्धेश् च[*]। न ह्यन्यभावं c.2221

[o-o] Ci Utp 37,11–12 [p-p] Ci NM I 77,10–11; TR 60,20–22 [q-q] Cie TBV 285,21; NMak 40,1–3 [r-r] Ci J 205,11 [s-s] HBṬ 147,28 [t] cf. above §§ c.111 and c.112

---

6 eka° n.e. T **7** tad eva n.e. T **18** eva n.e. T **19** ca n.e. T

[σ] tadanyad vā Utp; anyad NM, TBV for tato ’nyad [τ] tṛtīya° om. TBV

[1]प्रतिपद्य पुनस्[*] तत्प्रतिपत्तेरन्वयव्यतिरेकौ प्रसाध्य तदभावं ms 20b
प्रतिपद्यते। किं तर्हि। तदन्यं प्रतिपद्यमान एव तदभावं प्रत्येति,
[*]तद्दर्शनानन्तरमव्यवधानेन – इदमस्तीदं नास्तीति व्य[2]वसायात्, दृ-
ष्टान्तासिद्धेश् च। तच् च तस्य लिङ्गं भवति यस्य येनान्वयो ऽस्ति।
न ह्येवं शक्यं दर्शयितुं यत्रान्यभावोपलब्धिस् तत्र[*] तदभाव इति,
तदेकोपलब्धेः क्वचिद्[3]प्यन्यत्रा[*]भावात्। सामान्येन प्रदर्शने दृष्टान्ते
ऽपि प्रमाणान्तराभावात् सैव तदन्यभावोपलब्धिः साध्यधर्मस्य
साधिकेति दृष्टान्तानवस्थायामप्रतिपत्तिः॥

c.23 तस्मा[4]न् न कुतश्चिल् लिङ्गात् तदभावसिद्धिः। [u]सो ऽन्यभावः प्रत्य- T 84,1
क्षलक्षणेनानुपलम्भेन सिद्धो ऽभावव्यवहारं साधयेन् [*]मूढप्रतिपत्ता-
वि[u]त्यलं प्रसङ्गेन॥

4.31 सेयं त्रिविधा[5]नुपलब्धिः – सिद्धे कार्यकारणभावे सिद्धाभावस्य HBṬ 202,16
कारणस्यानुपलब्धिः, व्याप्यव्यापकभावसिद्धौ सिद्धाभावस्यैव[*] व्याप-
कस्यानुपलब्धिः, स्वभावानुपलब्धि[6]श् चेति। तत्र कारणव्यापकयोरपि
स्वभावासद्व्यवहारसिद्धिरन्यभावसिद्धिरेव। स तथासिद्धः कार्यव्याप्य-
योरभावमभावव्यवहारं वा साधयति। स्व[1]भावानुपलब्धौ तु व्यवहार ms 21a
एवानुपलब्ध्या लिङ्गभूतया साध्यते॥

4.311 यदि तर्हि[*] कारणव्यापकौ तदन्यभावसिद्धिरूपयानुपलब्ध्या सिद्धा- T 84,16 HBṬ 203,5
सद्व्यवहारावभावमन्यस्य [2]साधयतः, सा च तयोरुपलब्धिलक्षणप्राप्ता-

---

[u-u] **Re'** PVSV 4,20–5,1

---

1 punaḥ n.e. T **3** tat° n.e. T **5** tatra{da} ms **6** ‹anyatrā› ms, anyatra n.e. T
10 mūḍha° n.e. T **13** eva n.e. T **18** tarhi n.e. T

वेवासद्व्यवहारस्य साधिकेति, कथं तयोः परोक्षे ऽर्थे* प्रयोगः। नैव प्रयोगः प्रमाणतया लिङ्गानिश्चयात्। [3]केवलं सिद्धसम्बन्धयोः कारणव्यापकयोर्यद्यभावः परस्याप्य*वश्यमभावनिश्चय इति दर्शनार्थमेते प्रयुज्येते॥

HBṬ 204,27 इत्येष एव **पक्षधर्मो** ऽन्वयव्यतिरेकवा[4]न् इति **तदंशेन व्याप्तस्** त्रिलक्षण एव त्रिविध एव **हेतुर्**गमकः, स्वसाध्यधर्माव्यभिचारात्॥ 4.4

T 84,30 HBṬ 205,23 [vw]षड्लक्षणो [w]हेतुरित्य<u>परे</u>[uU] – त्रीणि चैतानि, अबाधितविष[5]यत्वं विवक्षितैकसङ्ख्यत्वं ज्ञातत्वं चेति॥ d.

तत्राबाधितविषयत्वं तावन् न पृथग् लक्षणम्, [xy]बाधाविनाभावयोर्विरोधात्[y]। अविनाभावो हि हेतोः साध्यधर्मे [6]सत्येव भावः। कथं च स* तल्लक्षणो धर्मिणि हेतुः स्यान् न चात्र साध्यधर्मो[x] भवेत्[v]। प्रत्यक्षानुमाने हि साध्यधर्मं बाधने प्रवृत्ते तं ततो धर्मिणो निवर्तयतस् त[ms 21b][1]स्मिन् सत्येव भवन् हेतुस् तं तत्र धर्मिणि प्रवर्तयतीति परं बत भावानामस्वास्थ्यं वर्तते॥ d.11

HBṬ 207,6 अन्यत्र साध्यधर्मेणाविनाभावी हेतुर्न *साध्यधर्मिण्येवेति चेत्, [z]तत् किमयं [V]तपस्वी ष[2]ण्ढमु[W]द्वाह्य पुत्रं मृग्यते[z]। यस्य धर्मिणि साध्यधर्मे*ऽसत्यपि भावस् तमुपदर्श्य कथं धर्मी साध्यधर्मवानित्युच्यते। d.111

---

v-v **Ci'e** PSṬ 2.5,1–5 w-w HBṬ 11,16 x-x **Ci'e** VNṬ 139,7–9 y-y cf. NVTṬ 36,13–14; 301,11; NM I 284,15; 293,1 z-z cf. NVTṬ 36,21; NM I 286,3–4

U ‹nayāyikamīmāṃsakādaya[ḥ]› gl. ms (HBṬ 205,23-24) V ‹varākaḥ› gl. ms
W ‹na puṃs nāliṅga› gl. ms

---

1 arthe n.e. T **3** api n.e. T **9** sa n.e. T **13** sādhya° n.e. T **15** °dharme n.e. T

---

u aparaḥ PSṬ for apare ms

अत एवाबाधामुक्तामिति चेत्, स्यादेतद् यत [3]एव हेतुरन्यथापि भवेत्, अत एव प्रमाणाभ्यामबाधिततद्धर्मा धर्मीत्युच्यत इति। [a]तत् किमिदानीं हेतोः सामर्थ्यमबाधयैव साध्यसिद्धेः[a], साध्याभावो हि बाधक[4]प्रमाणवृत्तिनियत इत्यबाधायां साध्यसिद्धिरिति व्यर्थो हेतुः। बाधायामपि साधनसामर्थ्याभावात्। अनियमे न च बाधकं प्रमाणं स्यात् साध्याभावस्य च [5]सम्भव इति नाबाधायाः सामर्थ्यम्॥

d.112 न च बाधाऽभावो ऽबाधा। किं तर्हि बाधानुपलब्धिः। सा पुरुषस्य T 86,27 HBṬ 209,2 क्वचिद् बाधासम्भवे ऽपि स्यादिति स हेतुप्रयोगविषयः। किं नु वै हे[6]तुर्बाधोपलब्धेर्बिभेति न बाधायाः, येन बाधामनादृत्यानुपलब्धौ प्रयोग इष्टः। स तर्हि हेतुः परमार्थतो बाधाया भावमभावं वा ऽनपेक्ष्य बाधाऽनुपलब्धौ [1]प्रयोक्तव्यः। स[*] किमर्थं प्रयुज्यते। साध्यसिद्ध्यर्थम्[*]। ms 22a स किं क्वचिद् बाधायामपि सत्यां साध्यं साधयेद् येनास्या नाभावनिर्णयं प्रति यत्नः क्रियते हेतुश् च प्रयुज्यते। तथापि [2]नाबाधितविषयत्वं हेतुलक्षणम्, बाधायामप्यस्य सामर्थ्यात्। तथा च यथानुपलम्भे बाधाया भावसम्भवे ऽप्यभ्युपगम्य प्रयोगः संशयितस्यानभ्युपगमे [3]प्रवृत्त्ययोगात्, तथा बाधोपलब्धावपि प्रयोगः, अभ्युपगमे सति[*] विशेषाभावात्॥

d.1121 न बाधायां समर्थ इति चेत्, यद्येवं नानिर्णीत[*]बाधाऽसम्भवः प्र[4]योगमर्हति – मा भूत् प्रयुक्तस्याप्यसामर्थ्यमिति। T 88,13

[a-a] Ci NVinV II 179,15–16

---

11 sa n.e. T » bsgrub par bya ba'i phyir T for °siddhyartham **16** sati n.e. T **18** anirṇīta° em. (HBṬ 210,17; gtan la ma bab par T) : nirṇṇīta° ms

HBṬ 210,14 बाधाऽनुपलम्भे सामर्थ्यमिति चेत्, किमुपलम्भो बाधां व्याप्नोति, d.1122 येन तन्निवृत्तौ बाधानिवृत्तिर्यतो हे[5]तोर्बाधासम्भवकृतमसामर्थ्यं न स्यात्। तथापि व्यर्थो हेतुर्बाधाऽनुपलम्भादेव साध्यसिद्धेः, अनुपलम्भे बाधाऽसम्भवात्। उपलम्भनिवृत्तावपि बाधाऽनि[6]वृत्तौ तदवस्थं हेतोरसामर्थ्यमित्यप्रयोगः। तस्मात् स्वसाध्यभावाभावाभ्यामन्यथापि भवन् धर्मिणि हेतुर्न किञ्चिद् भावयति न विभावयतीति न तदुपक्षेपः* ms 22b समर्थः।[1] [b]तन् न बाधाऽविनाभावयोः सहभावः। तेन नाबाधा रूपान्तरम्[b]॥

T 88,28 HBṬ 212,2 तन् नाम तस्माद् विशेषणान्तरं स्याल् लक्षणान्तरत्वेन वोपादानम- d.12 र्हति, यद्भावे ऽपि यस्यान्यथाभावः, तद्यथा पक्ष[2]धर्मत्वं सपक्षे च भाव इति। न चैतदबाधाया* अविनाभावे सति सम्भवतीति न हेतुविरुद्धयोः साध्यविपर्ययाविनाभाविनोर्विषये बाधा सम्भव इति न तद्[3]भावः पृथगनयोर्लक्षणत्वेन वाच्यः। तस्मान् न हेतुप्रयोगे सति* प्रतिज्ञादोषाणां सम्भवः। नापि केवलायाः प्रतिज्ञायाः प्रयोगो ऽस्तीति न प्रतिज्ञादोषा [4]वाच्याः॥

T 90,8 HBṬ 213,6 एतेनैकसङ्ख्याविवक्षापि प्रत्युक्ता। [c]कथमेको हि स्वसाध्यभाव एव भा- d.21 वात् तेनाव्यभिचारी। तत्रैव तदन्यो ऽपि तद्बाधकस्य भाव* एव भावाद् विरुद्धस् ते[5]ने[c]ति बाधया समानम्॥

अपि च [d]यो वस्तुतो ऽसम्भवत्प्रतिहेतुः, स किं सम्यग्ज्ञानविपर्यय- d.22 हेतुरिष्टः[d], आहोस्विदप्रदर्शितप्रतिहेतुः। किं चातः॥

[b-b] Ci'e PSṬ 2.5,5–6 [c-c] Ci'e PSṬ 2.5,11–13 [d-d] HBṬ 218,4–5

---

6 tadupakṣepa<ḥ> em. (HBṬ 211,23) : tadupakṣepa□ ms 11 caitad a{vyava}-bādhāyā ms (gnod pa srid pa 'di ni T) 13 sati n.e. T 17 bhāve n.e. T

d.221 यद्यसम्भवत्प्रतिहेतुः, अ[6]लक्षणमेतदशक्यनिश्चयत्वात्। [e]हेत्वभावो (T 90,16 HBṬ 214,1) वा[*e]। न ह्यनिश्चितात्मनः प्रतिपादकधर्मस्य तल्लक्षणत्वं संदिग्धपक्षधर्मत्ववत्, नापि संदिग्धलक्षणो हेतुरिति, न कश्चिद् धेतुः[1] स्यात्। (ms 23a) [f]तुल्यलक्षणे हि [f]दृष्टः प्रतियोगिसम्भवो ऽदृष्टप्रतियोगिष्वपि शङ्कामुत्पादयति, विशेषाभावात्। सति वा* विशेषे स एव* हेतुलक्षणम्। ततो हि हेतुरे[2]कान्तेन निरस्तप्रतिपक्षः स्वसाध्यं निश्चाययतीत्यतल्लक्षणो न हेतुः स्यात्। तथा चैकसङ्ख्याविवक्षा व्यर्था। अतो विरुद्धाव्यभिचारिलक्षणं हीयेत –[3] [g]स्वलक्षणयुक्तयोर्हेत्वोरेकत्र* विरोधेनोपनिपाते विरुद्धाव्यभिचारी[g]ति। न च तस्य विशेषस्य रूपं निर्दिश्यते, यत् प्रतीत्य प्रतियोगि[4]सम्भवासम्भवावुत्पश्यामः। तस्मान् नास्त्येव विशेष इति सर्वत्र शङ्कया भवितव्यम्। दृष्टप्रतिहेतोरपि हेतोः प्रागितरेण न कश्चि[5]द् विशेषो लक्ष्यते। न च सम्भवत्प्रतिहेतूनामपि सर्वदा तदुपलब्धिः, अतिशयवती तु प्रज्ञोत्प्रेक्षणी दृष्टा। तेनानिश्चयः सम्भवासम्भवयो[6]रित्यनिश्चितलक्षणत्वान् न कश्चिद् धेतुः स्यात्॥

d.2221 अथाप्रदर्शितप्रतिहेतुर्हेतुः, यथाह – [h]यदा तर्हि शब्दत्वं नित्यमभ्यु- (T 92,8 HBṬ 218,6) पै[1]ति, तदायं हेतुरेव स्यात्, यद्यत्रानित्यत्वहेतुं कृतकत्वादिकमपि क- (ms 23b) श्चिन् न निर्देशयेदति[h]। इदमिदानीं कष्टतरं व्यसनमापतितमप्रकाश्यमसंवरणीयं च क[2]थं निर्वोढुं शक्येत। [i]स तावदयं हेतुर्वस्तूनि स्वसाध्यतत्त्वप्रकृतीनि कृत्वा तत्प्रमाणकान् पुरुषानभ्युदयनिःश्रेयसाभ्यां

---

e-e HBṬ 214,22–23; 216,11 f-f HBṬ 217,18 g-g **Cee** PSV on PS 3.23b (cf. Steinkellner 2013: II, note 226); **Ci'e** PSṬ 2.5,8–10 h-h **Ce** PSV on PS 3.24cd (PSV¹ 50a8–50b1; PSV² 133a5–6) i-i **Ci'e** NVinV II 180,3–6

1–2 gtan tshigs med pa yaṅ ma yin te T for hetvabhāvo vā **5** vā n.e. T » sa eva n.e. T **8** chos can gcig la T for ekatra

संयोज्य पुनः प्रतिभावता* [3]पुरुषेण हेत्वन्तरनिदर्शनोत्कीलितसाध-
नसामर्थ्यस् तानि वस्तूनि तांश् च पुरुषांस् तद्भावसम्पदः प्रच्याव्य
भ्रष्टराज्य इव राजा तपोवनं [4]गच्छती[i]ति किमत्र ब्रूमः ॥

HBṬ 219,14 पुरुषप्रतिभाकृते च साधनत्वे किमिदानीं* वस्तुतः साधनमसाधनं d.2222
वा। [j]स च हेतुः स्वभावतस् तद्धर्म[5]भावी कथमन्यथा क्रियते, [k]वस्तूनां
स्वभावान्यथाभावस्य विरुद्धोभयस्वभावस्य चाभावात्[k], अतद्धर्मभावी
च कथमन्यदापि साध[6]नं कस्यचित् ॥

T 92,30 तस्मात् स्वभावतः स्वसाध्याविनाभाविनोर्विहितलक्षणयोः कार्य- d.23
ms 24a स्वभावयोस् तल्लक्षणस्य प्रतिहेतोरभा[1]वादलक्षणमेकसङ्ख्याविवक्षा[j],
व्यवच्छेद्याभावात् ॥

HBṬ 220,20 [l]ज्ञानं* पुनरलिङ्गधर्मः। कथं लिङ्गस्य लक्षणं स्यात्। किंरूपाल् d.3
लिङ्गादर्थः प्रतिपत्तव्य इति चिन्तायां प्रति[2]पत्तुरविसंवादकस्य रूपमु- d.31
च्यते, यद्दर्शनादयं साधनासाधने प्रविवेच्य तस्येष्टार्थसन्निधान[φ]प्रत्य-
यात् प्रवर्तते। तत्र यदस्यात्मरूपं तल् लक्षणं न पररूपं* [3]प्रतिपत्ति-
जन्मन्युपयोगमात्रात्, तल्लक्षणत्वे ऽतिप्रसङ्गात्। एवं हि प्रमेयपुरुषा-
दीनामपि तल्लक्षणत्वं स्यात्, न हि तेष्वप्य*सत्सु लिङ्गि[4]नि ज्ञान-
मि[l]ति ॥

T 94,15 HBṬ 222,4 निश्चितग्रहणं[m] तर्हि न कर्तव्यम्। न न कर्तव्यम्, तस्यान्यार्थत्वात्। d.311

[j-j] **Ci'e** PSṬ 2.5,13–6,4 [k-k] cf. TSP 895,12 [l-l] **Ci'e** PSṬ 2.6,7–7,1 [m] cf. PVin 2.9c

---

1 yaṅ phyir khyod kyis T for punaḥ pratibhāvatā **4** idānīm n.e. T **11** śes pa ñid T for jñānam **14** pa‹ra›rūpaṃ ms **16** api n.e. T

[φ] ° sādhana° PSṬ for °sannidhāna

d.3111 *सपक्षविपक्षयोर्दर्शनादर्शनाभ्यां गमकं हेतुमिच्छतां नैवं* सम[5]र्थो हेतुर्भवति, दर्शनादर्शनयोः सतोरप्यगमकत्वात्*। तेन भावाभावाभ्यां गमक इति ज्ञापनार्थं निश्चितग्रहणम्। तेन न पररू[6]पं लक्षणम्, लिङ्गरूपविशेषस्य तेनानभिधानात्। तौ हि भावाभावौ *तद्भावसाधनप्रमाण*वृत्त्या बोद्धव्यौ, उपायान्तर[1]स्यासम्भवात्। तेन तयोः प्रदर्शना- ms 24b य निश्चितशब्दः प्रयुक्तो लक्षणे, यद्यपि* भावाभाववचनमात्रेणापि [n]तत्साधनप्रमाणवृत्तिरा*क्षिप्य[2]ते[n]। अन्यथा तयोरेव सत्ताऽप्रसिद्धेः, ज्ञानसत्तानिबन्धनत्वाज् ज्ञेयसत्ताव्यवस्थायाः – सर्वत्र सत्ताव्यवस्थैव प्रमाणं तत्साधनमन्वा[3]कर्षतीति। परार्थत्वाच् च शास्त्रप्रणयनस्य – त्रिरूपं लिङ्गं वः* संवादकमर्थस्येति। तद् रूपं ये न विदन्ति न तेषां ततः प्रवृत्तिरिति [4]परोपलक्षणत्वादेव* ज्ञानं सिद्धमिति, तथापि तावेव भावाभावौ <u>केचिद्</u> दर्शनादर्शनमात्रेण व्यवस्थापयन्तीति तन्निषे[5]धार्थो निश्चितशब्दः, सतोरपि भावाभावयोरन्वयव्यतिरेकयोः सत्तासंशयात्। °यतः प्रमाणादनयोर्निश्चयः, तदधीना[6]सत्ताप्रसिद्धिरिति ज्ञापनाय निश्चित*वचनं कृतम°<u>स्माभिः</u>॥

---

n-n HBṬ 224,5–6 o-o cf. HBṬĀ 408,21–23

---

1 sapakṣavipakṣayoḥ n.e. T » kho na T for evam 2 śes par byed pa ñid ma yin pa mthoṅ ba'i phyir T for agamakatvāt 4 tadbhāva° em. (HBṬ 223,9; de'i ṅo bo T) : tadabhāva° ms 4–5 °pramāṇa° n.e. T 6 yady api n.e. T 7 °vṛttir n.e. T 10 vaḥ n.e. T 11 eva n.e. T 15 niścita° n.e. T

T 96,13 HBṬ 225,13 ms 25a यतो ऽपि भावाभाववचनमात्रेण तत्साधनप्रमाणाक्षेपसिद्धिः [1]पृथग् अतो न ज्ञानं लक्षणम्[*], तेनैव[X] गतत्वात्[*], उपनयार्थवत् पक्षधर्मत्वात्। d.32

HBṬ 225,21 [p]अन्वयव्यतिरेकयोरपि तर्हि न पृथक्त्वम्[p], एकस्य प्रयो[2]गादुभयगतेरिति चेत्, न, हेतोः[*] [q]सपक्षविपक्षयोर्भावाभावयोरपरस्परापेक्षत्वात्[q]। एकं वाक्यमुभयं गमयतीत्युच्यते, नैको ऽर्थो [3]द्वितीयस्य। ननु [r]तत्रैव भावस्[*] तदभावे ऽवश्यमभावश्[r] च परस्परमाक्षिपतः। वचनमेतदुभयं सामर्थ्यादाक्षिपति, एकस्यापि नि[4]यमख्यापकस्य द्वितीयाक्षेप[*]नान्तरीयकत्वात्। न पुनः केवलौ भावाभावौ परस्परमा[*]क्षिपतः, नियमवन्तौ च न केवलौ, [5]नियमस्योभयरूपत्वात्[*]। तस्मात्तत्रैव भाव इति न भाव एवोच्यते, नेतरेणाप्यभाव एव, येन भावो ऽभावो वा द्वितीयमाक्षिपे[6]त्। नैवं ज्ञानम्, परोपलक्षणात्[*] [s]त्रैलक्षण्याद्व्यतिरेकादि[s]ति न लक्षणान्तरम्॥ d.321

---

p-p HBṬ 226,26–27 q-q HBṬĀ 409,18–19 r-r cf. HBṬ 226,19–21 s-s cf. HBṬ 228,26–27

X ‹niścitagrahaṇenaiva› gl. ms

1–2 <pṛthag ato na jñānaṃ la>kṣaṇam em. (cf. de'i phyir yaṅ śes pa ni mtshan ñid tha dad par gyur pa ma yin te | T) : $_1$///kṣaṇaṃ ms **2** don rtogs pa'i phyir T for gatatvāt **4–5** prayo<gād ubhayagater iti cet, na, hetoḥ> em. (sbyar bas gñi ga stogs pa'i phyir ro źe na | ma yin te | ... gtan tshigs T) : pray[o] /// $_2$///sapakṣa° ms **6–7** <dvitīyasya | nanu tatraiva bhāva>s em. (gñis pa ... ‖ de kho na la yod pa T) : $_3$///s ms **8–9** ni<yamakhyāpakasya dvitīyā>kṣepa° em. (ṅes pa ston pa ... phen pa gñis pa ... T) : ni $_4$///kṣepa° ms **9** parasparam n.e. T **10** <niyamasyobhayarūpatvā>t em. (ṅes pa ni gñi ga'i ṅo bo yin pa'i phyir ro ‖ T) : $_5$///t ms **12** ākṣipe<t, na evaṃ jñānam, paropalakṣa>ṇāt em. (cf. śes pa ni de ltar gźan śes par byed pa'i ... ma yin no ‖ T) : ākṣipe $_6$///ṇāt ms

(d.) तस्मान् न हेतुः षड्लक्षण इति ॥ T 98,3

0.3 हेतुबिन्दुर्नाम प्रकरणम् $_{1}$आचार्यधर्मकीर्तिकृतं समाप्तम्। *कृतिरा- ms 25b
चार्यस्याशेषविदः श्रीधर्मकीर्तेः ॥

---

2 prakara<ṇam ācāryadharmakīrtikṛtaṃ samāptam |> kṛtir em. : prakara $_{1}$/// kṛtir ms

Diplomatic Edition

HB 1b

1b1 ◌ namo mañjunāthāya ‖ parokṣārthapratipatter anu-
mānāśrayatvāt* | saṃkṣepatas tadvyutpādanārtham idam ā-
rabhyate ‖ pakṣadharmmas tadaṃśêna vyāpto ¦

1b2 hetus tridhaiva saḥ | avinābhāvaniyamād dhetvā¦⊙bhā-
sās tato 'pare ‖ pakṣo dharmmī | avayave samudāyopacārāt' |
prayojanābhāvā

1b3 d anupacāra iti cet* | na | sarvvadharmmidharmmaprati-
ṣe¦⊙dhārthatvād upacārasya | evaṃ hi cākṣuṣatvādiparihṛ-
taṃ bhavati | dharmmavacanenāpi dharmmyāśra¦

1b4 yasiddhau | parāśrayatvād dharmmasya | dharmmivaca-
{tva}¦⊙nā[t*] pratyāsatteḥ sādhyadharmmisiddhir iti cet^{0} |
na | dṛṣṭāntadharmmiṇo pi pratyāsatteḥ | tadaṃ

1b5 śavyāptyā | dṛṣṭāntadharmmiṇi satve siddher ddharmmi-
dharmma⊙vacanāt sādhyadharmmiparigrahaḥ | siddhe pu-
narvacanaṃ niyamārtham āśaṅkyeta | sajātīya eva sa¦

1b6 •••••••••••••••••••••••• [sādhyābhāve 'sattvavacanavad
dharmmidharmma]vacanam* | siddhe pi dṛṣṭāntadharmmi-
ṇi bhāve tadaṃśavyāptivacanāt* | •••••

HB 2a

2a1 bhāvaniyamārtham āśaṅkyeta | tatsāmarthyād arthagatāv upacāramātrāt samānanirdeśāt pratipattigauravañ ca parihṛtam bhavati |॥ pakṣasya dharmmatve tadviśe

2a2 ṣaṇāpekṣasyānyatrānanuvṛtter asādhāraṇate⊙ti cet* | na | ayogavyavacchedena viśeṣaṇāt* | yathā caitro dhanurddhara iti | nānya

2a3 yogavyavacchedena | yathā pārtho dhanurddhara i⊙ti |॥ tadaṃśas taddharmmaḥ | vyāptir vyāpakasya tatra bhāva eva | vyāpya‡sya vā tatraiva bhāvaḥ |

2a4 etenānvayo vyatireko vā yathāsvaṃ pramāṇe⊙na niścita ukto veditavyaḥ | pakṣadharmmaś ca | sarvvatra hetāv asatā sādhyadharmmeṇa he¦

2a5 tor vvyāptya□siddheḥ | avyāpakasya vā nivṛttau nivṛttyabhāvād iti | anvayavyatirekābhyāṃ niścitābhyān tadaṃśavyāptir nniścitā bhavati | tatra pa

HB 2b

2b1 kṣadharmmasya sādhyadharmmiṇi pratyakṣato 'numānat{au}o vā prasiddhir nniścayaḥ | yathā pradeśe dhūmasya śabde vā kṛtakatvasya | sadhūmaṃ hi prade□śam arthāntaravi

2b2 viktarūpam asādhāraṇā[tma]nā dṛṣṭavataḥ pratyakṣe⊙ṇa yathādṛṣṭabhedaˇ‹[ya]dā niścayaṃ janayati | tadaiva pramāṇaṃ |› paramārthaviṣayaṃ ‡‡ smārttaṃ liṅgajñānam utpadyate | tatra tad ādyam asādhāraṇaviṣa above l. 1+2?

2b3 yan darśanam eva pramāṇam* | tasmi[ṃs] tathābhūte dṛṣṭe ⊙ sa yena yenāsādhāraṇas tadasādhāraṇatān tato bhedam abhilapantī smṛtir utpannā pratyakṣa¦

2b4 balenātad[vyāvṛ]ttiviṣayā yathādṛṣṭākā[ragra]haṇâ⊙n na pramāṇam* | prāg asādhāraṇaṃ dṛṣṭvā 'sādhāraṇam ity abhilapato 'pūrvvā[rth]ādhigamābhā¦

2b5 vāt* | arthakriyāsādhanasya darśanāt* | adṛṣṭasya tatsādhanasya punaḥ svabhāvasya vikalpenāpratipatteś cānumānavat* | arthakriyārthī hi sarvva‹ḥ› pra in l. 5

HB 3a

3a1 māṇam apramāṇaṃ vā 'nveṣate prekṣāvān* | na ca sā-
mānya kāñcid arthakriyām upakalpayati | svalakṣaṇapra-
t[i]patter ūrddhvan tatsāmarthyotpannav[i]

3a2 kalpajñānagrāhyam* | yathā nīlan dṛṣṭvā nīlam i⊙ti jñā-
ne | tad eva hi nīlasvalakṣaṇam* □ tathāvidhasādhyārthakri-
yākāri | tac ca tenā

above l. 1 3a3 tmanā pratyakṣeṇa dṛṣṭaˇ‹adhyavasāyaṃ kurvat' pra-
t[y]akṣaṃ pra[mā]•• ••›m eva | na ca tatsvalakṣaṇa⊙graha-
ṇottarakālabhāvino nīlavikalpasya viṣayeṇa nīlasādhyārtha-
kriyā sādhya¦

3a4 te | tasmād anadhigatārthaviṣayaṃ pramāṇam ity a¦⊙py
anadhigate svalakṣaṇa iti viśeṣaṇīyam* | adhigate svalakṣa-
ṇe tatsāmarthyajanmâ

3a5 vikalpas tadanukārī kāryatas tadviṣayatvāt* ⊙ smṛtir eva
na pramāṇam* | anadhigatavasturūpānadhigateḥ | vastvadhi-
below l. 6 +5 ṣṭhānaˇ‹rūpa›tvāt pramāṇa

3a6 vyavasthāyāḥ | arthakriyāyogyaviṣayatvāt tadarthipravṛ-
tteḥ | arthakriyāyogyalakṣaṇatvād vastunaḥ | tato pi vika-
below l. 6 lpāt tad‹[svalakṣaṇa]›adhyavasāyena vastuny? eva?¦

HB 3b

3b1 pravṛtt[e]ḥ | pravṛttau ‹tu› vikalpasya pratyakṣeṇābhinnayogakṣematvāt* | pūrvvapratyakṣakṣaṇena ‡‡ kvacid abhinnopayogatvād uttareṣām aprāmāṇyaprasaṅga iti above l. 1

3b2 cet* | na kṣaṇaviśeṣasādhyārthavāñchāyāṃ ‡ nā⊙nāyogakṣematvāt* | sādhāraṇe hi kārye na teṣāṃ sāmarthyabhedaḥ | aparāparadhūma¦

3b3 pramitasannikṛṣṭāgnivad agnimātrasādhye rthe | e⊙tena dharmmidharmmaliṅgādivikalpasya pramāṇa‡pṛṣṭhabhāvinaḥ prāmāṇyaṃ ‡‡ pratyuktam* || ~ |

3b4 anvayaniścayo pi svabhāvahetau sādhyadharmmasya ⊙ vastutas tadbhāvatayā sādhanadharmmabhāvamātrānubandhasiddhiḥ | sā sādhyaviparyaye heto¦

3b5 r bbādhakapramāṇavṛttiḥ | yathā yat sat tat kṣaṇikam e⊙va | akṣaṇikatve arthakriyāvirodhāt* | tallakṣaṇa[ṃ] vastutvaṃ hīyata iti | kāryahetau kā¦

3b6 ryakāraṇa[bhāvasiddhiḥ] yathedam asyopalambhe upalabdhilakṣaṇaprāptam anupalabdham upalabhyate satsv apy anyeṣu hetuṣv asyābhāve na bhavatīti □ tadbhāve ¦

HB 4a

above l. 1 +1 4a1 bhāvo 'bhāve 'bhāvaś ca | pra˘‹trividha[ḥ]›tyakṣānupalambhasādhanaḥ □ kāryakāraṇabhāvaḥ | tasya siddhiḥ ˡ kāryakāraṇabhāva eva hy arthāntarasyaiva[ṃ] syād ya‡‡tra dhūma¦

4a2 s tatrāvaśyam agnir iti | agnibhāva eva hi bhāvo dhū⊙masya tatkāryatvam iti || anupalabdhāv apy asadvyavahārasyopalabdhilakṣaṇaprāptānupala

4a3 bdhimātravṛttisādhanam anvayaniścayaḥ | nimittāntarā¦⊙bhāvopadarśanāt* || o || vyatirekaniścayo pi kāryasvabhāvahetvoḥ kāryakāraṇavyāpya

4a4 vyāpakabhāvasiddhau | kāraṇavyāpakānupala⊙bdhibhyāṃ dṛśyaviṣayābhyāṃ sādhyābhāve hetvabhāvasiddhiḥ [|] uddiṣṭaviṣayasyābhāvasyopa

4a5 darśane | anupalabdhilakṣaṇaprāptasyānyathā ‡ kvacid abhāvāsiddheḥ | anu‡ddiṣṭaviṣayaṃ punaḥ sādhyābhāve 'bhāvakhyāpanaṃ pratibandhamātrasiddhau si¦

HB 4b

‹ca/va/ta □ eva/eda› above l. 1

4b1 dhyatīti na tatra dṛśyaviṣayatā anupalabdher vyatireka-sādhane apekṣyate ‖ vyatirekaniścayo ’nupalabdhāv upa-labdhilakṣaṇaprāptāt sato anupalambhā¦

4b2 [bhā]vadarśanam* ‖ etallakṣaṇas tridhaiva sa hetus tri-¦⊙prakāra eva | svabhāvaḥ | kāryam anupalabdhiś ceti | yathā a!nitye kasmiṃścid gamye satvaṃ |

4b3 agnimati pradeśe dhūmaḥ | abhāve ˇ‹abhāvavyavahāre› below l. 5 +3
copalabdhila⊙kṣaṇaprāptasyānupalabdhir iti | [a]sminn eva triprakāre a!vinābhāvaniyamāt* | yatho

4b4 ktā vyāptir avinābhāvaḥ pakṣadharmmasya | na sa tri-vi⊙dhād dhetor anyatrāstīty atraiva niyata ucyate ‖ ˇ‹|•• ••||› below l. 5
tatra sādhanadharmmabhāvamātrānvayi{•i}ni sādhya

4b5 dha[r]mme svabhāvo hetuḥ | vastuto liṅgisvabhāva evāparāparâvyāvṛttyā dharmmabhede pi | hetusvabhāve ’nvayavyabhicārābhāvād viśeṣaṇaṃ lakṣaṇe

HB 5a

5a1 tanmāt[r]ānvayena paramatāpekṣam* | pare hy arthāntaranimittam ata[dbh]āvamātrānvayinam api˴ dharmmaṃ svabhāvam icchantīti | viśeṣaṇena tathāvidha[syā]tatsvabhāvatāṃ

5a2 tasmin* sādhye hetor vyabhicārañ cāha | yathā vi⊙nāśe hetumati kṛtakatvasya || tasya dvidhā prayogaḥ | sādharmmyeṇa vaidharmmyeṇa ca | yathā ya

5a3 t sat tat sa[r]vvaṃ kṣaṇikam* | yathā ghaṭādayaḥ | saṃ⊙ś ca śabda iti | tathā kṣaṇikatvābhāve satvābhāvaḥ | yathā vandhyāsute | saṃś ca śabda iti

5a4 sarvvopasaṃhāreṇānvayena vyatirekeṇa {vā} ca vyâ⊙ptipradarśanalakṣaṇau sādharmmyavaidharmmyaprayogau || atra sāmarthyād eva pratijñārtha

5a5 pratīter nna pratijñāprayogaḥ | apradarśite pra⊙meye kathaṃ tat°pratītir iti cet* | svayaṃ pratipattau kaḥ prameyasya darśayitā | prade

5a6 śasthaṃ dhūmam upalabdhavatas tasyāgninā vyāptismaraṇe tatsāmarthyād evāgnir atreti bhavati | na ca tatra kaścid agnir atrety asmai nivedayati | nāpi ¦

HB 5b

‹•• •• •› above l. 1 +3

5b1 svayaṃ prāg eva pratipadyate kiñciˇ‹•• ••›t* | pramāṇam above l. 1
antareṇaivaṃ pratīter nnimittābhāvāt* | pratītau vā liṅgasya
vaiyarthyāt* | svayam evākasmād agnir atreti

5b2 prameˇ‹prat•jñāṃ?›yaṃ vyavasthāpya ‡ punas tat*prati- above l. 1 +2
pattaye liṅga¦⊙m anusaratīti ko yaṃ pratipattikramaḥ |
pareṇāpi tad ucyamānaṃ plavata evopayogābhâ

5b3 vāt* | viṣayopadarśanam upayogaś cet* | tenai⊙va tāvad
darśitena ko rthaḥ | yadi pratipattir anyathā na syāt* ‡‡
sarvvaṃ śobheta | tasmād eṣa{ḥ}

5b4 svayaṃ pratītau viṣayopasthāpanena kenacid vinā⊙pi
pratiyann asmān* kāryiṇo dṛṣṭvā | parvvabrāhmaṇa iva
vyaktaṃ mūlyaṃ mṛgayate | asmadvacanâ

5b5 d api svayaṃ siddham eva liṅgam anusṛtya pratyetīti ⊙
ko 'nayor avasthayor vviśeṣaḥ | dṛṣṭā ca pakṣadharmma-
sambandhavacanamātrāt pratijñāvaca

5b6 nam antareṇāpi pratītir iti kas tasyopayogaḥ | svaniśca-
yavad anyeṣān niścayotpādanāya ca sādhanam ucyate | ta-
trāyaṃ svayaṃ prameyopadarśana¦

HB 6a

above l. 1 +2 ‹•• ••›

6a1 m antareṇāpi pratipadya paraṃ pratipādayann apūrvvam arthakramam āśrayata iti kim atra kāraṇam* | tasmān na
above l. 1 +1 prameyavacanena kiñcit* | anya□thāpi ˇ‹tat'›pratipa

6a2 tter utpatter iti | etenopanayanigamanādi¦○kam api pra-
above l. 1 +2 tyuktam* | etāvataiva ‹dvyavayavavākyenaiva› prayogeṇa pratītibhāvād iti | ḍiṇḍikarāgaṃ parityajyā¦

above l. 1 +3 6a3 kṣiṇī nimīlya cintaya tāvat* kim iyatā ‹pakṣadharmma-sambandhavacanamātrakeṇa› pratīti○ḥ syān na veti | bhāve vā kiṃ prapañcamālayā | itīyān eva sādhanavākyaprayogo jyāyān⁰ ¦

6a4 || atrāpi na kaścit pakṣadharmmasambandhavacana-
in l. 4 {yoḥ}‹pra○yoga›kramaniyamaḥ ˡ sarvvathā gamakatvāt* | sambandhavacane pi prayoga eva bhidyate nārthaḥ | u

6a5 bhayathā dharmmabhede pi tadbhāvasyaiva khyāpanāt* | ○ na hy ekāntenātatsvabhāvasya bhāve aˡnyabhāvaḥ | kṛta-katvabhāva iva praya□tnotpa¦

6a6 ttidharmmatāyāḥ | nāpy atatsvabhāvasya nivṛttau tanni-vṛttir akāryasya | yathānayor eva dharmmayor vviparya-yeṇa | tasmād anvayavyatirekayor yathālakṣa

HB 6b

6b1 ṇam eko pi prayukto dvitīyam ākṣipati iti naikatra sādhanavākye dvayoḥ ‹anvayavyatirekayo[ḥ]› prayoga iṣyate ꞁ vaiyarthyāt* | tat*svabhāvatayā tadanvayasiddhau tadabhāve above l. 1 +(1)

6b2 aꞌbhāvasiddheḥ | tadabhāve aꞌbhāvasiddhau ca tadanva⊙yasiddheḥ | tadabhāva evābhāvakhyātir yathā syān nānyatra na? viruddha iti niyamakhyāpanā¦

6b3 rtho pi vyatirekaprayogo na yukto 'nyaviruddhayô⊙r api vipakṣatvāt* || katham idānīṅ gamyate sato 'vaśyan naśvaraḥ svabhāva iti yenānvayavya

6b4 tirekau syātām* vināśahetvayogāt* | svabhâ⊙vata eva bhāvā naśvarā naiṣāṃ niṣpa□nnānām anyato nāśotpattis tasyāsāmarthyāt* | na hi

6b5 vināśahetur bhāvasvabhāvam eva karoti | tasyā⊙nyato 'bhinirvṛtter nāpi svabhāvāntarakaraṇe ‹tadava›sthasya ‹bhāvasya› kiñcid iti tathopalabdhyādiprasaṅgaḥ | in l. 5 below l. 6 +5

6b6 nāpi svabhāvāntaram asyāvaraṇam* | tadavasthe tasminn āvaraṇasyāpy ayôgāt* | nāpi vi□nāśahetunā bhâvābhāvaḥ kriyate | abhāvasya vidhinā kārya¦

HB 7a

7a1 tvopagame vyatirekāvyatirekavikalpānatikramāt* | bhāva[pratiṣedha]rūpatve ca bhāva‡n na karotīti syāt* | tathā cākarttur ahetutvam iti | na vi‡‡nāśahe

7a2 tuḥ kaścit* || vaiyarthyāc ca | yadi svabhāvato naśva⊙ro bhāvas tasya na kiñcin nāśahetunā | svayan tatsvabhāvatayaiva nāśāt* | yo hi yasya svabhā¦

7a3 vaḥ sa svahetor evotpadyamānas tādṛśo bhavati ⊙ | na punas tadbhāvê hetvantaram apekṣate | prakāśadravoṣṇakaṭhinādidravyavat* | na hi prakāśādaya

7a4 s tadātmāna utpannāḥ punaḥ prakāśādibhāve he¦⊙tvantaram apekṣante | tadātmanas tādātmyābhāve nairātmyaprasaṅgāt* | tadvad asthitidharmmā cet* svabhā

7a5 vato bhāvo niṣpannaḥ punar nna tadātmatāyāṃ hetva-
below l. 6 +5 nta⊙ram apekṣeta | ‹atra paraḥ prāha |› bījādivad anekānta
below l. 6 +5 iti cet* | ‹siddhāntavādī prāha› syād etat* | bījādayo 'ṅkurāder jananasva¦

7a6 bhāvāḥ santo pi na kevalā janayanti ˌ śalilādikāraṇāntarāpekṣatvāt* | tadvad bhāvo pi vināśe syād iti | na ˌ tatsvabhāvasya jananāt* | ajanakasya cāta¦

HB 7b

7b1 tsvabhāvatvāt* | ata eva tayor avasthayor vvastubhedo
niśceyaḥ | bhāvānāṃ svabhāvānyathātvābhāvāt* | tatsva-
bhāvasya paścād iva prāg api jananaprasaṅgāt* | tasmād yô

7b2 'ntyo 'vasthābhedaḥ sa evāṅkurādijananasvabhāvaḥ | ⊙
pūrvvabhāvinas tv avasthāviśeṣāḥ kâraṇakâraṇānīti nāne-
kāntaḥ | kṣaṇikeṣu bhāveṣv ˇ‹nirantaragatya•ā› aparāpa above l. 1

7b3 rotpatter aikyābhāvāt* | te 'ntyāḥ samarthāḥ kin na ⊙ ja-
nayantīti cet* | janayanty eva nātrānyathābhāvaḥ | svabhā-
vāvaiparītyāt* | teṣu sarvveṣu saha¦

7b4 kāriṣu samarthasvabhāveṣu ko 'parasyopayo¦⊙ga iti cet*
| na vai bhāvānāṃ kācit* prekṣāpūrvvakāritā | yato 'yam
eko pi samarthaḥ kim a

7b5 trāsmābhir ity apare nivartteran* | te hi nirabhiprā-
ya⊙vyāpārāḥ svahetupariṇāmopanidhidharmmāṇas tatpra-
kṛtes tathābhavanto nopālambham arha¦

7b6 nti | samarthāḥ kin na aparāparaṃ janayantīti cet* | na ¦
tatrai‸‹vā•• mya?›vaikatra sāma□rthyāt* | tasyaivaikasya ja- below l. 6
nane samarthā nānyasyeti nāparāparajananaṃ || bhinnasva

HB 8a

above l. 1 / above l. 1 +1   ‹•• •• •• •• •• •• •• •• ••›   ‹•• •• •āntarayoḥ›

8a1 bhāvebhyaś cakṣurādibhyaḥ sahakāribhya ekakāryotpattau na kāraṇabhedāt kāryabhedaḥ syād iti cet* | na ǀ yathāsvaṃ svabhāvabhedena tadviśeṣopayoga

8a2 taḥ | tadupayogakāryasvabhāvaviśeṣāsaṅkarā⊙t* | yathā mṛtpiṇḍakulālasūtrādibhyo bhavato ghaṭasya mṛtpiṇḍād amṛtsvabhāvebhyo vṛkṣādibhyo

8a3 bhinnaḥ svabhāvaḥ | kulālât tasyaiva mṛdātmanaḥ sa⊙taḥ saṃsthānaviśeṣātmatayā tadanyebhyo bhinnaḥ | sūtrāt tasyaiva mṛtsaṃsthānaviśeṣātmanaś ca

8a4 krāder vibhaktaḥ svabhāvo bhavati | tad evaṃ na kulā¦-⊙lān mṛtsvabhāvatā na mṛdaḥ saṃsthānaviśeṣaḥ | na ca tayoḥ śaktiviśeṣaviṣayabhede pi tajja¦

8a5 nitaviśeṣabhedasya kāryasya svabhāvabhedaḥ | mṛtsaṃsthānayor aparasparātmatayā ǀ saṃsthānamṛtsvabhāvaviśeṣābhyāṃ tayor apratibhāsanaprasaṅgāt* | ˇ‹vaiśeṣikaḥ prā-

below l. 5 +4! / below l. 5   ha› anyaˇ‹•• •o syāt›

HB 8b

8b1 d eva saṃsthānaṃ guṇo mṛddravyāt* | tena bhinna‹ḥ› in l. 1
svabhāva‹ḥ› kulālamṛtpiṇḍayor upayogaviṣaya iti cet* | in l. 1
uktam atra | api ca yadi tatsaṃsthānaṃ bhinnaṃ mṛdaḥ ku

8b2 lālaḥ kin na pṛthak karoti | guṇasya dravyapāratantryā-
⊙n na pṛthak* siddhir iti □□□| ˇ‹paro bauddhamatam ā- above l. 1 +2
śāṅkyāha{•• ••}› tatsaṃsthānādhārātmakaṃ tad dravyaṃ
saṃsthānaṃ vā tadādheyātmakaṃ prakṛtyâ

8b3 kiṃ kulālam apekṣanta iti cet* | na | tataḥ para⊙spara-
sambandhayogyatāpratilambhāt* | anyathā prāg api mṛtpi-
ṇḍasya saṃsthānaviśeṣasambandha

8b4 yogyatve vastudharmmatayaiva saṃsthānaviśeṣasa⊙m-
bandhaprasaṅgaḥ | eva{ṃ} ‹(bauddhaḥ prāha)› n! tarhi sā below l. 5 +4
yogyatā mṛddravyasya kulālāt* | na cānayoḥ svabhāvabhe-
daḥ |

8b5 bhede vā | pūrvvavat* prasaṅgād iti | asti tāvat kiñcid
ekasvabhāvatve py anekapratyayopahitasvabhāvaviśeṣam
iti | na nirbbandho ‸‹asmākaṃ› mṛtsaṃsthānayor ekasva¦ below l. 5 +5

HB 9a

9a1 bhāvatvasādhane | tena sahakāriṇaḥ pratyayā naikopayogaviṣayāḥ kāryasyaikasvabhāvatve pi vastuta iti ‖| yatheha kāraṇabhedo bhinnaviśeṣopayogā

9a2 n naikakāryaḥ | tathā cakṣurādibhyo pi jñānotpattā⊙v unneyaḥ | tathā hi samanantarapratyayād vijñānāc cakṣurvvijñānasyopalambhātmatā | tasyaivôpalambhā¦

9a3 tmanaḥ sataś cakṣurindriyād rūpagrahaṇayogyatā¦⊙pratiniyamaḥ | viṣayāt ta[ttu]lyarūpateti | abhinnatve pi vastutaḥ kāryasya kāraṇānāṃ bhinnebhyaḥ

9a4 svabhāvebhyo bhinnā eva viśeṣā bhavantīti na kāra⊙ṇabhede py abhedas tat*kāryaviśeṣasyeti | ta evaite kāraṇaśaktibhedā yathāsvaṃ prativi¦

9a5 śiṣṭakāryajanane ’vyavadheyaśaktitayā pratyupa⊙sthitāḥ kṣaṇikatvāt sāmagrīkāryasya svabhāvasthityāśraya ity ucyante | tathā hi tat tebhyaḥ sama

9a6 stebhya upalambhātmakaṃ rūpagrahaṇapratiniyataṃ viṣayarūpañ ceti | prativiśiṣṭasvabhāvam ekaṃ jātam iti ‖|
below l. 5 ‹(atrāpi paraḥ)› apratirodhaśaktikeṣv anantarakāryeṣu kṣaṇikeṣv a{h}

HB 9b

9b1 nādheyaviśeṣeṣu pratyayeṣu parasparaṃ kaḥ sahakārā-
rtha iti cet* | na vai sarvvatrātiśayotpādanaṃ sahakriyā kin
tarhi! ekārthakaraṇam api yad bahūnām* | yathāntya¦

9b2 sya kāraṇakalāpasya | ‹kasmāt'› tad eva mukhyaṃ saha- below l. 6 +2?
kāriṇāṃ ⊙ sahakāritvam* | tasyaivāntyasya kāraṇatvāt* |
tatra ca kṣaṇe! ekasya svabhāvasyāvivekād ‹abhedāt'› vi above l. 1 +2

9b3 śeṣasya karttum aśakyatvāt* | svabhāvāntarotpatti¦⊙la-
kṣaṇatvād viśeṣotpatteḥ | bhāvāntaraprasavasambhave ca
nāntyaḥ syāt* | tataś ca na sākṣā¦

9b4 t*kāraṇaṃ syāt* | tasmān na kāraṇasya sahakāri⊙bhyo
viśeṣotpattiḥ | te samarthā eva svabhāvato 'ntyāḥ pratya-
yāḥ saha jāyante kṣaṇikā

9b5 yeṣāṃ prāk[p]aścāt* pṛthagbhāvo nāsti | yato 'na⊙-
ntaraṃ kāryotpattis tatraikārthakriyaiva sahakāriṇāṃ saha-
kāritvam* | samarthaḥ kuta utpanna i

9b6 ti cet* | svakāraṇebhyus tāny enam aparapratyayasanni-
dhāna eva kiñ janayanti | kadācid anya□thāpi syuḥ | tataś
caikô pi kvacij janayed iti cet | aparāpara

HB 10a

10a1 pratyayayogena pratikṣaṇaṃ bhinnaśaktayaḥ santanva-
in l. 1 ntaḥ saṃskārā‹ḥ› । yady api kutaścit sāmyāt sarūpāḥ pra-
tīyante । tathāpi bhinna evaiṣāṃ svabhāvaḥ | tena kiñcid
eva kasyacit kāra

10a2 ṇam* || tatra yo 'vyavadhānādideśarūpêndriyādikalâ⊙-
paḥ sa vijñānajanane samartho hetuḥ | yas teṣāṃ paraspa-
ropasarppaṇādyāśrayaḥ pratyayaviśe

10a3 ṣaḥ sa taddhetujanane samarthaḥ | teṣāñ ca na pūrvvan
na paścā⊙n na pṛthag bhāva iti samarthān api pūrvvāpara-
pṛthagbhāvabhāvino doṣā nopalīyante | tenaiṣāṃ

10a4 parasparopasarpaṇādihetur yaḥ sa samarthahetu¦⊙r iti
tasya na kadācid apy anyathābhāvaḥ | anena nyāyena sa-
rvvatra hetuphalabhāvapratiniyama

10a5 unneyaḥ || pratikṣaṇam aparāparasvabhāvabhedānvayi-
below l. 5 +5 nīṣu bhāvaśaktiṣu □ na sthiraikasvabhāveṣu ‹bhāveṣu› sva-
bhāvānyathātvābhāvāt* | samarthāsamarthasvabhāvayoḥ
kriyā¦

HB 10b

10b1 kriyāyogāt* || anyasahitaḥ karoti na kevala iti cet^{0} | kiṃ
kevalasya ˇ‹sva›kāryajananena samarthaḥ svabhāvaḥ | ‡ above l. 1
samarthaḥ | kin na karoty | akurvvan* kathaṃ samarthaḥ |
ku¦

10b2 vindˇ‹tantravāpa›ādayaḥ paṭādikaraṇe samarthā api na above l. 1
sarvvadā ⊙ kurvvantīti cet* | krīḍanaśīlo devānāṃ‡‡priyaḥ
sukhaidhitaḥ kṛtaṃ kṛtaṃ punaḥ kārayati | tathā

10b3 hi bījādyupanyāse nirloṭhitam etat* | tasmāt tatsva⊙bhā-
vasyānyathātvābhāvāt* | taddharmmaṇas tathābhāvo 'ntyā-
vasthāvad anivāryo 'ntyāvasthāyāṃ prāg a¦

10b4 samarthasya sāmarthyôtpattau tatsāmarthyasya tatsva-
bhāvatve ⊙ apūrvvotpattir eva sā ‹|›'tatsvabhāvatve so 'kā- in l. 4
raka eva sāmarthyākhyāt padārthāntarāt kāryotpatteḥ |

10b5 api ca sa tadaiva tāvat* ˇ‹sannihita›sakalasahakārī below l. 5 +5
kāryaṃ kiṃ karoti | kurvvan* dṛṣṭas tena karotīti brūmaḥ |
mahāsāmarthyaṃ ‹mahāprabhāvasya bhavato› darśanaṃ in l. 5
‹paramatam āśaṅkāt^{0}› | yad idaṃ bhāvān ata¦ below l. 5

HB 11a

11a1 tsvabhāvān api svabhāva‡mātreṇa citrêṣu vyāpāre ni-
above l. 1 +1 yu[ṅkte] | yadi nāma ‹kadācit'› kiñcit kathaṃcid atra
above l. 1 +1 bhavato darśanaviṣayam ‹patha iti kvacit pāṭhaḥ |› atikrā-
med ˡ dhanta aprasavadharmmakam apetasantānaṃ ¦

above l. 1 +2 11a2 syād itīyaṃ naś cintā cittaṃ dunoti ‹kṣiṇotīti kvacit'› |
above l. 1 +2 na vai ‹vilakṣya prāha› vayam ata¦⊙tsvabhāvānāṃ bhā-
vānām asmaddarśanāt kāryakriyāṃ brūmaḥ | kin tarhi tat*-
kriyādharmmāṇaḥ svabhāva¦

11a3 ta [e]va te tān* paśyanto vidmas ta ete kārakā iti | ⊙
satyam ˡ idam apy asti | svabhāvas teṣāṃ kāryakriyādha-
rmmā | tena na samastapratyayānāṃ kāryam akṛtvo

11a4 pekṣāpattir iti | sa kiṃ teṣām akṣepakriyādharmmâ sva-
bhāvas tadaivāntyāvasthāyām utpanna āhoś¦vit* prāg apy
āsīt* | āsīt* | apracyutotpannasthiraika¦

HB 11b

11b1 svabhāvānāṃ bhāvānāṃ kadācit* kasyacit* svabhāvasyābhāvavirodhāt* | tat* kim idānīṃ mātā ca vandhyā ca | ‡‡‡ ko vāsya bhāṣitasyārthaḥ | akṣepakriyāsvabhāvo

11b2 na karoti ca [| sa]hitas tatsvabhāvô na kevala iti cet^{0} ⊙ | anyas tarhi kevalaḥ | anyaḥ sahitaḥ | svabhāvabhedalakṣaṇatvād bhāvabhedasya | na hi sa sāhitye

11b3 pi pararūpeṇa karttā | svarūpañ cāsya prāg api tad e¦⊙veti kathaṃ kadācit* ‸‹kārya›kriyāvirāmaḥ | yasyāpi kṣaṇiko bhāvas tasyāpi kin na kevalaḥ karo¦ — above l. 1 +3

11b4 ti | karoty eva yadi kevalaḥ syāt* kin na bhavati ˈ kṣa⊙ṇikatvāt* | uktam atra yādṛśasya kriyā sa katham ekakṣaṇabhāvyānyathā syāt* | yaś ca bhavati sa {sa}

11b5 eva na bhavatīti [n]āyaṃ prasaṅgaḥ | kārakākārakayoḥ svabhāvataddhetvor vvirodhāt* || yo pi manyate akṣepakriyādharmmaiva sa tasya svabhāvô na ‸‹sa› sāhityam a — below l. 5 +5

HB 12a

12a1 pekṣate | kāryan tu pratyayāntarāpekṣam iti sahitebhya eva jāyate na kevalebhya iti | tasyāpi kathaṃ sa kevalo pi karoty eva kāryañ ca tasmān notpadyata i

12a2 ti | tadavasthô virodhaḥ || na kevalaḥ karoty e[v]eti ⊙ cet* | katham i{ā}dānīm akṣepakriyādharmmā svabhāvaḥ | nanv etad eva paridīpitaṃ bhavati | karo¦

12a3 ty eveti | [k]āryañ cāyaṃ kevalo pi samarthaḥ san* ⊙
above l. 1 +3? param apekṣamāṇaṃ katha[m u]pekṣeta ˇ̭‹param anādṛtyaitat prasahya ku[r]yāt' |› | evaṃ hy anena sātmanaḥ sāmarthyam api darśitaṃ bhavati | kā

below l. 6 +4 12a4 [r]ya[ṃ] param apekṣata iti ˇ̭‹tataḥ› kevalād anutpattir uktā bha⊙vat[i] | sa kevalo pi samarthasvabhāva iti tata utpattir iti | ete cai[katra] kathaṃ [sy]ātām* | tad aya

12a5 m īrṣyāśalyavitudyamānamarmma viklavam*‡ vikrośatī⊙ty upekṣām arhati ||| tasmād idam ekārthakriyālakṣaṇaṃ
below l. 6 +5 sahakāritvaṃ kṣaṇikānām eva bhavānāṃ ˇ‹sambhavat[i]› na sa

12a6 mbhavat*pṛthagbhāvānām akṣaṇikānām* || pṛthak⁰karaṇasambhavena sahakāritvaniyamāyogāt* || yatra tu [sa]ntānopakāreṇa bhāvāḥ pratyayatāṃ pratipadyante |

HB 12b

12b1 yathā taṇḍulabījādibhya odanāṅkurādijanmani dahanodakapṛthivyādayaḥ | tatra viśeṣotpādanaṃ pratyayānāṃ sahakriyā santānāśrayeṇocyate | na dravyāśra¦

12b2 yeṇa | kṣaṇike dravye viśeṣānupapatteḥ | na hi ta¦⊙ṇḍulādīnāṃ dahanodakādibhyaḥ krameṇa svabhāvātiśayānutpattāv odanādyabhinirvṛttir asti |

12b3 indriyasya vā prabhāsvarād avavarakaṃ pravṛṣṭasya svo¦⊙pakāribhyaḥ svasantānaviśeṣānutpattāv arthapratipattijananam* | akṣeˇ‹avilambita›pakāriṣu punar indri¦ below l. 5 +3

12b4 yādiṣu na parasparato viśeṣotpattiḥ | tatra yathâ⊙svaṃ pratyayaiḥ parasparôpasarppaṇādyāśrayair ye yogyadeśādyavasthā [j]ātās te saha svabhāva

12b5 niṣpattyā jñānahetutāṃ pratipadyanta ity ekārthakriyaiva sahakāritvam* | yatra tu viśeṣôtpādanena sahakāriṇāṃ pratyayatvaṃ tatra hetusaṃtānasya pratyayā

HB 13a

13a1 ntarāpekṣeti tataḥ svabhāvāntarapratilambha ucyate |ǁ tatra svarasataḥ pūrvvakṣaṇanivṛttau hetupratyayānāṃ tebhya eva viśiṣṭ{e}akṣaṇaviśeṣotpattiḥ | krameṇātiśayavato ¦

above l. 1 +2 13a2 'ntyāt kā‡‡raṇakalāpāt* kāryotpattiḥ |ǁ ‹paraḥ prāha› sahakā⊙riṇaḥ samutpannaviśeṣāt kāraṇāt kāryôtpattau viśeṣasyaivotpattir nna syāt* | aviśiṣṭād viśeṣô

13a3 tpattau kāryasyāpi syāt* | tataś ca parasparato vi¦⊙śeṣotpādânapekṣiṇaḥ sahakāriṇaḥ kāryaṃ ‡ kuryuḥ | tenākṣaṇikānām api sahakāryape¦

13a4 kṣiṇāṃ kāraṇatā syāt* | na cāpekṣyebhyaḥ svabhāvā⊙tiśayotpattiḥ | atha viś{o?}eṣotpattāv api sahakāriṇā kṛtaviśeṣa evôpatiṣṭhet* | anavasthai

13a5 vaṃ syāt* | na ca sahakāriṇo nityaṃ parasparasya kāryotpādānuguṇaviśeṣotpādanayogyāvasthāḥ | yena nityānuṣakta evaiṣāṃ parasparakṛto viśeṣaḥ syāt* |

HB 13b

13b1 tadupāyāpāyayoḥ kāryavyaktivirāmadarśanāt* | tenādyo viśeṣaḥ sahakāribhyo nirupakārasya notpadyeteti || ‹bauddhaḥ prāha› nāsmākaṃ punaḥ punar vvacanê kaścid udvegô yady e above l. 1 +1

13b2 vam api lokasya nyāyapratipattiḥ syāt punar api brūma⊙ḥ | na viśeṣotpādanād eva ‸‹sahakāriṇāṃ |› sahakāritvaṃ yena tadabhāvād viśeṣotpattāv asahakāriṇaḥ syuḥ | above l. 1 +2

13b3 kin tarhy ekārthakriyāpi | sāpi na bhaven nirvviśeṣā¦⊙ṇāṃ parasparataḥ | bhāve vā tadavasthāyām iva pṛthag api syāt* | tathā ca tad viśeṣabhāvi kāryam api

13b4 kevalāt syād iti cet* || sarvvam uktam* | pratikṣaṇam apa⊙rāparaiḥ pratyayair yathā bhāvasantāne □□ viśeṣotpattiḥ | yogyadeśatādyavasthābhedāḥ kāryakā

13b5 riṇaḥ | teṣāñ ca yata utpattiḥ | pratyekaṃ sāmarthye pi □ yathā kevalānām akriyākartṛviśeṣapṛthagbhāvābhāvāt* | kāryadvaividhyañ ca ı sahakārijanitaviśeṣapa

HB 14a

14a1 ramparôtpattidharmmakam* | anyac ca | aṅkurādivat* |
above l. 1 akṣepakārīndriyā□□vijñānāˇ‹di›vac ca | kāryakāraṇa[sva]-
bhāvabhedād iti | tatra sahakāribhyaḥ santānopakārāpekṣa

above l. 1 +2 14a2 kāraṇakāryajanmany ādyaḥ ˇ‸‹sahakāriviśeṣaḥ | na›
sahakārikṛtaviśeṣa[janmâ] ⊙ ’nantarakāryavat* | tataḥ pra-
above l. 1 +2 bhṛti ye viśeṣās te tajjanmā{ā}nas tatprakṛtiˇ‹ka›tvāt* | tasya
teṣāṃ ceti nānava

14a3 [sthā] | tathā yady akṣaṇiko pi [bh]āvo ’nāhitātiśayaḥ
above l. 1 +3 sa⊙hakāriṇādyaviśeṣa‹hetu›vat kāryaṃ kurvvīta ‡ | karotu |
sa punar asya svabhāvo ’kṣepakartṛdharmmā cet* | pṛtha

14a4 gbhāvasambhavāt* | kevalo pi tathā syād ity uktam* |
ata⊙tsvabhāvas tu tadāpy akāraka eva | tasmān nākṣaṇike-
ṣu hetuṣv ekārthakriyā kasyacit* sahakāritva

14a5 niyamo nāpi santānopakāreṇ{ô}eti na tasya kaścit* ⊙ sa-
hakārī tataḥ kevalo pi kuryād iti | prāyas tu saṃghātasthāyī
bhāvasantānaḥ sahakāripratyayo

14a6 pajanitaviśeṣaḥ svakāryaṃ kurvvan* dṛṣṭo bījādivad iti |
in l. 6 sthirahetuvādinaḥ ‹pratyayāntarā›pekṣā vyaktaṃ kāraka-
svabhāvāntarotpattir iti | nākāryasyāpekṣety ucyatê |

HB 14b

14b1 kārakasvabhāvasya prāg api bhāve ‹’›kriyā’yogāt* | in l. 1
tasmād yo yadātmā sa svasattāmātreṇa tādṛśo bhavati | na
ca bhūtvā punas tadbhāve a¦parābhisaṃskāram apekṣata iti
¦ svabhā¦

14b2 vato ’sthitidharmmaṇo bhāvasya na kiñcin nāśakāraṇaiḥ
| ⊙ sthitidharmmaṇo pi kenacit svabhāvānyathābhāvasya
karttum aśakyatvāt* | kin nāśakāraṇaiḥ | anyathātvapra

14b3 tipattau vā tatsvabhāva eva na syād iti ‡ pūrvvo vi-
kalpas tatra ⊙ coktam* | yaś ca parasmād anyathābhāvaḥ so
’paraḥ svabhāvaḥ | ˟‹yaś cāparaḥ sa kathaṃ tasya› svabhā- above l. 1 +3
vabhedalakṣaṇatvād bhāvabhedasya | ta

14b4 thā ca pūrvvako bhāvo ’pracyutidharmme sthita iti na
tasyā¦⊙nyathābhāvaḥ | ‹pratyākhyati |› etena kaṭhinādīnāṃ below l. 6 +4
tāmrādīnām agnyādibhyo dravatvādisvabhāvāntarotpattiḥ
pratyu

14b5 ktā | tatrāpi pūrvvakasya svarasanirodhitvād vināśe ¦⊙
saty agnyāder upādānāc câpara eva dravasvabhāva utpanna
iti | sa svayaṃ sthitidharmmaiva vināśahetva

14b6 sambhave ’vasthānāt* | tasya parasmād vināśo ¦ ‹paraḥ below l. 6 +6
prāha› na ca vināśo nāmāparaḥ svabhāvaḥ | bhāvapracyutir
eva vināśa iti | ‹bauddhaḥ prāha› nedam uttaraṃ vikalpa- below l. 6 +6
dvayam atikrāmati ¦ kin nityo bhāvaḥ

HB 15a

15a1 svabhāvata āhoś!vid anitya iti vikalpe prāṅ nityo bhūtvā paścā[d] anityo bhavā!tīti bruvāṇo bhāvadvayaṃ {a?}nityānityasvabhāvabhedam* | pūrvvakasya nityābhimatasya svayaṃ nā¦

15a2 śam anāśaṃ ca sarvvadā prāha □ ity asamarthaḥ pūrvvasmin ‹pakṣe› vi¦⊙nāśahetuḥ | ‹nṛyonisa? evāha› na prāṅ nityo bhūtvā paścād anityo bhavati | kin tarhi paścād api nitya eva | ekasvabhāvatvā

above l. 1 +2
above l. 1 +2

15a3 t* | sa tarhi bhāvaḥ svabhāvena vināśam anāviśan* katham ⊙ naṣṭo nāma | tatsvabhāvavināśayoḥ parasparaparihārarūpatvāt* | tasmāt saty asya vināśe vināśa

15a4 svabhāvenaivānena bhavitavyam* | tathāpi vyartho vināśahe⊙tur ity uktam* | tena svabhāvato naśvare a!naśvare vā bhāve na vināśahetor upayogaḥ | tasmād vinā¦

15a5 śe 'napekṣo bhāvas tadbhāvaniyata iti yaḥ san* sa vinā¦⊙śī | naśvaratānivṛttau ca sattvanivṛttir iti | anvayavyatirekasiddhiḥ || svabhāvato naśvaratve pi kaścid ata

15a6 tsvabhāvo pi syāt* | na hi sarvvaḥ sarvvasya svabhāva iti nānvayavyatirekasiddhir iti cet* | na | akṣaṇikatve 'vastutvaprasaṅgāt* | śaktir hi bhāvalakṣaṇaṃ sarvvaśaktiviraho 'bhāvala

HB 15b

15b1 kṣaṇam* | na cākṣaṇikasya kvacic chaktiḥ | kramayaugapadyābhyām arthakriyāvirodhāt⁰ | tasmād yat sat tat* kṣaṇikam eveti vyāptisiddhiḥ || ‹1040?› || arthāntarê gamye kāryahetur a¦ in l. 1

15b2 vyabhicārāt* | kāryakāraṇabhāvena gamakatve liṅgasya ¦ ⊙ sarvvathā gamyagamakabhāvaḥ | sarvvathā janyajanakabhāvād iti cet* | na | tadabhāve bhavatas tadutpattini

15b3 yamābhāvāt* | tasmāt kāryaṃ svabhāvair yāvadbhir avinābhā⊙vi kāraṇe teṣāṃ hetus tatkāryatvaniyamāt* | tair eva ca dharmmair ye tair vvinā na bhavanti | aṃśena janyajana

15b4 katvaprasaṅga iti cet* | na | tajjanyaviśeṣagrahaṇe a¦bhi⊙matatvāt⁰ | liṅgaviśeṣopādhīnāñ ca sāmānyānām* | aviśiṣṭasāmānyavivakṣāyāṃ vyabhicā

15b5 rān neṣyate | kasyacit kadācit kutaścid bhāve pi sarvvas tā⊙dṛśas tathāvidhajanmeti kutaḥ | tathā ca nānvayavyatirekāv iti cet* | na | atadbhāvinaḥ sakṛd api ta

15b6 to ’bhāvāt* | parasparāpekṣayā janyajanakasvabhāvalakṣaṇe hi kāryakāraṇe | tatra yadi dhūmo ’gnyādisāmagryā anyato pi bhavên na tasya tajjanyaḥ svabhāva iti sa

HB 16a

16a1 kṛd api ta[to] na bhaved arthāntaravat* | nāpi sāmagrī taṃ janayed atajjananasvabhāvatvāt* sāmagryantaravat* | na ca dhūmasya tadatajjanyaḥ svabhāvo yukta ekasvabhāvatvāt* |

16a2 dhūmādhūmajanana svabhāvād bhavato dhūmādhūmasvabhāva¦⊙ḥ syāt* | kāryasvabhāvānāṃ kāraṇasvabhāvakṛtatvāt* | akāraṇāpekṣaṇe vā 'hetukatvapra¦

16a3 saṅgāt* | tasmāt* so 'gnyādisāmagrīviśeṣo yo ⊙ dhūmajanakaḥ sa dhūmô yo 'gnyādisāmagrīviśeṣaja‡nita ‡‡ iti
above l. 1 +3 kāryakāraṇayor evaṃ ‸‹svabhāva›niyamâ

in l. 4 16a4 n na vijātīyād utpattiḥ | ‹ta[n na dṛṣṭaṃ]› kāryaṅ kāraṇaṃ vyabhicara⊙ti | tena siddhe kāryakāraṇabhāve kāryasya kāraṇena vyāptiḥ siddhā bhavati || nanu vijātīyād a¦

below l. 6 +5 16a5 pi kiñcit* bhavad dṛṣṭaṃ tad yathā gomayā˅‹(ādiśabdāt' sūryamaṇicandrakāntyādeḥ |)›deḥ śālūkādiḥ | na ⊙ vijātīyād utpattiḥ | tathāvidham eva hi kāraṇaṃ tādṛśām ādi□□-nimittam iti na kāraṇabhedaḥ | prabandha

16a6 vṛttau tu śarâd bhāvaḥ | asti ca gomayetarajanmanoḥ svabhāvabhedo rūpābhede pi | na hy âkārasāmyam eva bhāvānāṃ tattve nibandhanam* | abhinnākārāṇām api ke¦

HB 16b

16b1 ṣāñci d anyato viśeṣāj jātibhedadarśanāt* | anyathā hi vilakṣaṇāyā api sāmagryā avilakṣaṇasyotpattau na kāraṇabhedābhêdābhyāṃ kāryabhedābhedau | ity ahe

16b2 tukau viśvasya bhedābhêdau syātām* | tathā hi na bhedā⊙d bheda ity abhedād api nā[bhe]daḥ | tadvyatiriktaś ca na kaścid bhāvasvabhāva ity ahetukatvād bhāvānāṃ nityaṃ sa

16b3 tvam asatvaṃ vā syād apekṣyâbhāvāt* | apekṣayā hi bhā⊙vāḥ kādācitkā bhav[anti] vyavasthāvāṁś ca sādhyeṣu sādhananiyogo na syāt* | kāraṇaśaktiprati

16b4 niyame hi kiñcid eva kasyacit* sādhanāyopādīyeta ⊙ nāparam* | tasyaiva tatra śakteḥ | anyasya cāśakteḥ | tayos tajjananetarasvabhāvatvêna bhedāt* | ta

16b5 jjananasvabhāvavilakṣaṇād api tasyotpattau na tajja⊙nanaśaktipratiniyamaḥ | iti yat* kiñcit* yata{śca}ḥ kutaścit* syāt* | tajjananaśaktisāmye tu tad e

16b6 veti na kāryaṃ dṛṣṭaṃ kāraṇaṃ vyabhicarati || ~ || [u]palabdhilakṣaṇaprāptasyānupalabdhir abhāvahetur abhāvavyavahārahetur vvā | atropalabdher upalabhamānadharmmatvê

HB 17a

above l. 1 17a1 ta˘‹j›jñānam upalabdhis tasmād anyopalabdhir anupalabdhiḥ | vivakṣitopalabdher anyatvāt* | abhakṣāsparśa‡nīyavat* paryudāsavṛttyā | upalabhyamānadharmmatve viṣayasvabhāva upalabdhi

17a2 ḥ svaviṣayavijñānajananayogyatālakṣaṇaḥ | yogyatāyā bhāvarūpatvāt* | tasmād anya upalambhajananayogya eva sv{ā}abhāvo 'nupalabdhiḥ pūrvvavat* | yatra yasminn upalabhyamāne

17a3 niyamena yadupalabdhir bhavati yogyatāyā aviśeṣāt* ¦ ⊙ sa tatsaṃsṛṣṭaḥ | ekajñānasaṃsarggāt tayoḥ sator naikarūpaniyatā pratipattir asambha‡vāt* | tasmād aviśi

17a4 ṣṭayogyatārūpayor ekajñānasaṃsargiṇoḥ parasparâ⊙pekṣam evānyatvam [i]heṣṭaṃ | sa kevalas tadapekṣayā tasmād anyas tajjñānan ta‡tsvabhāvô vā jñātṛjñeyadharmmala

17a5 kṣaṇā 'nupalabdhiḥ | sā 'bhāvam abhāvavyavahāraṃ vā pratiyo⊙ginaḥ sādhayati | katha[m anya]bhāvas tadabhāvo yenānyabhāvarū{pa••}pānupalabdhyā 'bhāvavyavahāraḥ sā¦

17a6 dhyate [|?] uktam atra | yathā paryudāsavṛttyā 'pekṣāto
in l. 6 ‹'›bhāvānupalabdhī | na pratiṣedhamātram ihānupalabdhiḥ | tasya sādhanāsiddher abhāvavyavahārāsiddhiprasaṅgāt* | tasyāsaṃsṛṣṭa

17a7 rūpasya bhāvasiddhir evāparasyābhāv{ā?}asiddhir ity anyabhāvo pi tadabhāva iti vyapadiśyate | anyabhāvalakṣaṇo 'bhāvaḥ svayaṃ pramāṇe‡na siddha{si}s tadabhāvavya‡va¦

HB 17b

17b1 hāraṃ sādhayet* ||| ˇ‹paraḥ prāha |› tatsiddhisiddho vā above l. 1
tadabhāva iti na kaścid viśeṣo yenānupalabdhyā 'bhāva-
vyavahārasiddhivirodhaḥ syāt* | sa evānyabhāvas tadviṣa-
yā copalabdhis ta

17b2 dabhāvasya ki[n n]a sādhanam* | kiṃ punar anyabhā-
vasiddhir eva ⊙ tadabhāvasiddhir iti || ‹(bauddhaḥ prāha)› above l. 1 +2
apṛthak°siddheḥ sambandhābhāvāc ca | anyabhāvas tāvan
na sādhanam* | yatsiddhau ya

17b3 sya na siddhiḥ, tat tasya liṅgaṃ bhavati dhūmāgnivat* |
anyabhāvasi⊙[ddhy]ai[va ta]dabhāvaḥ sidhyati | tasya
tadanyāsaṃsṛṣṭarūpasya kevalasya tatve vyavasthāpakād
eva pramāṇā¦

17b4 d anyavya[va]cchedasiddheḥ | [sambandh]ābhāvāc ca |
tac ca tasya liṅgaṃ ⊙ ‥‥t[i] | yena yasya [kaścit samb]a-
ndhô yathā [kṛta]katvāni[tyatva]yor ekārthasamavāyo |
dhūmasya vā svaliṅgi

17b5 [ny e]kārthasamavāya ādhārādheyabhāvo vā janya-
jana¦⊙kabhāvo vā | naivaṃ kaścid bhāvābhāvayoḥ samba-
ndho yenāsya sādhanaṃ syāt* | asti viṣayaviṣayibhā¦

17b6 vaḥ śabdārthava‡t* sambandha iti cet | na | śabdārthayos
tatpratipādanābhiprāye sati prayogā[t* tena saha]
kāryakāraṇalakṣaṇo 'vinābhāvalakṣaṇo vā sambandhaḥ
syā

HB 18a

above l. 1 +1 18a1 t* | ayañ ca prakāro ’tra na sambha‹va›ti kuto viṣayavi-
above l. 1 +1 ṣayibhāvaḥ | siddhe hi tayoḥ ˇ‹śabdārthayoḥ› sādhyasādha-
nabhāve tanmukhena viṣayaviṣayibhāvaḥ syāt* | sa evāsati
sambandhe na sidhyati

above l. 1 +2 18a2 taˇ‹sa[m]bandhās[i]ddhau›dasiddhau na viṣayaviṣayi-
bhāvaḥ | anyathetaretarāśra⊙yam idaṃ syāt* | anyabhāvāc
cābhāvasiddhau | asamudāyaś ca sādhyaḥ syāt* | tathā ca
ghaṭābhāvas tadanya¦

18a3 bhāvād iti ghaṭasya sarvvatra sarvvadā ’bhāvaḥ syāt* |
above l. 1 +? ‹paraḥ› na | pradeśā⊙didharmmiviśeṣaṇasyābhāvasya sā-
dhanād iti cet* | syād etat pra‡‡‡deśāder ddharmmiṇo viśe-
ṣaṇabhū

18a4 to ’bhāvaḥ sādhyate na kevalas tena nāsamudāyasā-
dhanam* | ⊙ na ca liṅgaliṅginor asambandho ’nyabhāvasya
pradeśādidharmmisambandhād iti | na | pradeśāder iva ta-
danya¦

18a5 bhāvatvāt* | yatraiva hi pradeśādau yan nāstīty ucyate sa
e⊙va tadasaṃsṛṣṭo nyabhāvas taddarśanād evāsya ghaṭo
nāstīti bhavati kathaṃ tasyaiva liṅgaliṅgibhāvaḥ | na cā

18a6 tra sāmānyaviśeṣabhāvavikalpaḥ saṃbhavati | yena sā-
below l. 6 mānyaṃ hetuḥ syāt* viśeṣo dharmmī | ‸‹na› tadviśeṣaprati-
below l. 6 +6 patter eva tadabhāvapratīteḥ | tasya cā‸‹nyatrāna›nvayāt* |
pratijñārthaikade

HB 18b

18b1 śatvāc cāliṅgatvam* | na ca yatra pradeśamātraṃ tatra
ghaṭābhāvaḥ | ‹paraḥ› tādṛśê kevale pradeśe ’bhāva ˇ‹eveti above l. 1
above l. 1 +1
c[e]› iti cet* | naˇ‹bauddhaḥ›nu tasyaiva kaivalyam iti above l. 1 +1
ghaṭaviraha ucyate | sa ceha liṅgabhūtapradeśapratipa

18b2 ttāv eva siddhaḥ | kasyedānīn tal liṅgam anvayānu‹gamanañ ca› nira¦⊙rthakam* | tasmād anyabhāvo na sādhanam abhāvasya || asti sambandho virodhas || tato ’nyabhāvād abhāvasiddhi

18b3 r iti cet* | kena kasya virodhaḥ | anyabhāvena pratiyo-
⊙ginaḥ | kin nu vai pratiyo gī pramātum iṣṭo yena virodhaḥ
sambandho liṅgaliṅginoḥ | aˇ‹bauddhaḥ›bhāvas tu pra¦ above l. 1 +3

18b4 tiyogino ’nyabhāvena na virudhyate | sahāvasthānāt* | ta⊙smin* prameye katham virodho liṅgaliṅginor ity asambandha eva | atrāpy asamudāyasādhyatvaṃ tadavastham* |

18b5 nanv asati sambandhe tadabhāvānyabhāvayor anyabhāvagatyāpi ⊙ tadabhāvagatir nna syāt* | na vai kutaścit sambandhād anyabhāvas tadabhāvasya gamaka iṣyate | api tv anyabhâ

18b6 va eva tadabhāvaḥ | yathoktaṃ prāk* | tasyānanyasaṃsṛṣṭarūpasya kevalasyaikātmani vyavasthitasya tenātmanā pariccheda evāparasya vyavaccheda iti | tasya kaivalyam e

HB 19a

above l. 1 ‹•• ••›

19a1 vāparavaikalyam iti | tadanyabhāva eva tadabhāvaḥ | tadanyapratipattir eva ca tadapratipattir ucyate | anyathā tatparicchedena tadanyāvyavacchede tatpariccheda eva na syāt* | tadata¦

19a2 drūpayor avivekāt* | iti ı ya eṣa kasyacid darśanāt kva-
above l. 1 +2 ci¦⊙t prāptiparihārārthô vyavahāraḥ sa ˇ‹eva› na syāt* | na
above l. 1 +2 hy aˇ‹yam a›nalaṃ paśyann apy analam eva paśyati | yena
śalilārthī ta

19a3 tra na pravarttêt* | anupalambhena śalilābhāvaṃ pratipadyata iti ⊙ cet* | ko yam anupalambho nāma | yadi śalilopalambhābhāvaḥ ı sa katham abhāvaḥ kasyacit pratipattiḥ pra

19a4 tipattihetur vvā | tasyāpi kathaṃ pratipattiḥ | kasyacid api tasya ⊙ tadanyasya vā ’pratipattāv api svāpamadamūrcchāvyavadhānaparāṅmukhyāvasthādiṣu kin nābhāvapratipattir iti ¦

19a5 vicāritaṃ pramāṇaviniścaye | tasmād ayam analaṃ paśyann apy a¦⊙nalo yaṃ na salilam ity anadhyavasyan na tiṣṭhen na pratiṣṭheteti dustaraṃ vyasanam āpannaḥ | tata evaikadarśanād a¦

below l. 6 +6? 19a6 nyābhāvapratītir iti cet⁰ | katham ekaṃ paśyann ‹prekṣāvān⁰?› anyan nāstīti pratīyāt⁰ | tasyaiva kevalasya darśanād iti cet* | idam evāsmābhir ucyamānaṃ kim atra bhavataḥ paruṣam ivā

HB 19b

19b1 bhāti | tasmāt tīrādarśineva śakuninā dūraṅgatvāpi pu-
nar āgantavyam ity alam apratiṣṭhānadik*pratipattyā || ‹pa- above l. 1
raḥ prāha› yady ekaparicchedād eva anyasya vyavaccheda-
siddhir aviśeṣeṇānyasya

19b2 sarvvasya tatrābhāva‡siddhiḥ syāt* | na tulyayogyāva-
sthasyai⊙vopalabdhilakṣaṇaprāptasyānupalabdhir abhāva-
ˇ‹vyavahāra›sādhanīti □ viśeṣaṇañ cāvācyam* | anupala- above l. 1 +2
bdhilakṣaṇa¦

19b3 prāptānām api tatra vyavacchedāt* | eˇ‹bauddhaḥ›kātma- above l. 1 +3
paricchedāt tasya ⊙ tadanyātmavyavacchedo bhavati |
tadātmaniyatapratibhāsajñānāt* | na hi tadātmā tadanyātmā
| ity avyavacchede ‹’› after l. 3

19b4 nyātmanaḥ pravṛttinivṛttyor abhāva iti pūrvva‹ḥ› pra- in l. 4
saṅgaḥ | tañ ca de⊙śakālasvabhāvāvasthāniyataṃ tadātma-
nopalabhamānā buddhis tathātvapracyutim asya vyava-
cchinatti | evaṃ hi sa ta¦

19b5 yā paricchinno bhavati yady anyathābhāvo vyava-
cchinnas tathātvañ ca ta⊙syaiva bhavati nānyasya i!ty
anyathābhūtāt tathābhūtaṃ vyavacchindaty eva tat* pari-
cchinattīty ekapramāṇavṛttiḥ sarvvabhā

19b6 vān* dvairāśye vyavasthāpayati | tasyānvayavyatireka-
buddhihetutvenaiva sāphalyāt* | tadvyatiriktāśeṣavyava-
cchedavyāptisādhanād eva prakārāntarābhāvasiddhiḥ | ta-
sya tadanya¦

HB 20a

20a1 tayā 'vyāptau tena tadarthāvyavacchedāt' | punar bhāvāparicchedaprasaṅgāt* | tasmāt kvacit* pramāṇaṃ pravṛttaṃ tat* paricchinatti | tato 'nyad vyavacchinatti | tṛtīyaprakārābhāvañ ca sūcaya¦

20a2 tīti! ekapramāṇavyāpāra eṣaḥ | tathā hi kvacit pramāṇaṃ pra⊙vṛttaṃ tad eva tadanyasmād vyavacchinatti tasyaiva
above l. 1 +2 paricchedāt* | tadanyad eva ca tasmā˘‹t ta›danyasya tatrāparicchedāt* |

20a3 atas tad eva pramāṇaṃ prakārāntarābhāvaṃ sādhayati | tasmin ⊙ dṛśyamāne dṛṣṭatadanyatvena sarvvasya vyavasthāpanāt* | atadanyasyaiva ca tatvena vyavasthāpanāt* | ete

20a4 na kramākramādayo 'nyonyavyava‡cchedarūpā vyākhyātāḥ ⊙ | tad evam ekopalambhāt tasya tadanyātmano vyavacchedo bhavati | na taddeśakālayoḥ sarvvānyabhāvavyavacche

20a5 daḥ ¦ tasmād atadātmā ca syāt taddeśakālaś ca ¦ rasarūpādivat* | ⊙ tasmāt kvacit kadācit kasyacid abhāvasiddhir yathoktād evānupalambhāt syāt* || a‡nyabhāvaviṣayā punar upa

20a6 labdhis tadabhāvasya sādhikeṣṭaiva na punar liṅgatvenaiva | tatrāpy abhāvasya pṛthak⁰ sādhyatvê sambandhābhāvasya tulyatvāt⁰ | liṅgāvirbhāvakāla eva tadabhāvasiddheś ca | na hy anyabhāvaṃ

HB 20b

20b1 pratipadya punas tatpratipatter anvayavyatirekau prasādhya tadabhāvaṃ pratipadyate | kin tarhi tadanyaṃ pratipadyamāna eva tadabhāvaṃ pratyeti ‖| taddarśanānantaram avyavadhānenedam astīdaṃ nāstīti vya

20b2 vasāyāt* | dṛṣṭāntāsiddheś ca | tac ca tasya liṅgam bhavati yasya ye⊙nānvayo sti | na hy evaṃ śakyaṃ darśayituṃ yatrānyabhāvopalabdhis tatra {da} tadabhāva iti | tadekopalabdheḥ kvacid a¦

20b3 py aˇ‹nyatrā›bhāvāt* | sāmānyena pradarśane □ dṛṣṭāntê above l. 1 +3
pi pramāṇānta⊙rābhāvāt* | saiva tadanyabhāvopalabdhiḥ sādhyadharmmasya sādhiketi dṛṣṭāntānavasthāyām apratipattiḥ | tasmā

20b4 n na kutaścil liṅgāt tadabhāvasiddhiḥ | so ’nyabhāvaḥ pratyakṣala⊙kṣaṇenānupalambhena siddho ’bhāvavyavahāraṃ sādhayen mūḍhapratipattāv ity alaṃ prasaṅgena ‖ se{ntri}yan trividhā

20b5 nupalabdhiḥ siddhe kāryakāraṇabhāve siddhābhāvasya kāraṇa¦⊙syānupalabdhiḥ | vyāpyavyāpakabhāvasiddhau siddhābhāvasyaiva vyāpakasyānupalabdhiḥ | svabhāvānupalabdhi¦

20b6 ś ceti | tatra kāraṇavyāpakayor api svabhāvāsadvyavahārasiddhiḥ | anyabhāvasiddhir eva | sa tathāsiddhaḥ | kāryavyāpyayor abhāvam abhāvavyavahāraṃ vā sādhayati |‖ sva

HB 21a

21a1 bhāvānupalabdhau tu vyavahāra evānupalabdhyā liṅgabhūtayā sādhyate |ǁ yadi tarhi kāraṇavyāpakau tadanyabhāvasiddhirūpayānupalabdhyā siddhāsadvyavahārāv abhāvam anyasya ¦

21a2 sādhayataḥ | sā ca tayor upalabdhilakṣaṇaprāptāv êvāsadvya⊙vahārasya sādhiketi | kathaṃ tayoḥ parokṣe 'rthe prayogaḥ | naiva prayogaḥ ˡ pramāṇatayā liṅgāniścayāt* |

21a3 kevalaṃ siddhasambandhayoḥ kāraṇavyāpakayor yady abhāvaḥ pa⊙rasyāpy avaśyam abhāvaniścaya iti darśanārtham ete prayujyete ˡ| ity eṣa eva pakṣadharmmô 'nvayavyatirekavā

21a4 n⁰ ǁ| iti tadaṃśena vyāptas trilakṣaṇa eva trividha eva hetur gga⊙makaḥ ǁ svasādhyadharmmāvyabhicārāt* ǁ o ǁ
below l. 6 +4 ṣaḍlakṣaṇo hetur ity apare ˇ‹naiyāyaika|mīmāṃsakādaya[ḥ]› | trīṇi caitāni | abādhitaviṣa

21a5 yatvaṃ ꜝ vivakṣitaikasaṃkhyatvaṃ ꜝ jñātatvañ ceti | tatrābādhitavi⊙ṣayatvan tāvan na pṛthak* lakṣaṇam* | bādhāvinābhāvayor vvirodhāt* | avinābhāvo hi hetoḥ sādhyadharmme

21a6 saty eva bhāvaḥ | kathañ ca sa tallakṣaṇo dharmmiṇi hetuḥ syān na cātra sādhyadharmmo bhavet* | pratyakṣānumāne hi sādhyadharmmabādhane pravṛtte taṃ tato dharmmiṇo nivarttayataḥ ta¦

HB 21b

21b1 smin* saty eva bhavan* hetus taṃ tatra dharmmiṇi pravarttayatīti param [b]ata bhāvānām asvāsthyaṃ varttate |‖ anyatra sādhyadharmmeṇāvinābhāvī hetur nna sādhyadharmmiṇy eveti cet* | tat* kim ayaṃ taˇ‹varākaḥ›pasvī ṣa¦ above l. 1 +1

21b2 ṇḍham ‹na puṃs nāliṅga[ṃ]› u‡dvāhya putraṃ mṛgyate above l. 1 +2 | yasya dharmmiṇi sādhyadharmme 'saty a⊙pi bhāvas tam upadarśya kathaṃ dharmmī sādhyadharmmavān i[ty] ucyate | ata evābādhām uktām iti cet* | syād etad yata ¦

21b3 eva hetur anyathāpi bhaved ata eva pramāṇābhyām abādhitata[ddh]a⊙r[mm]ā dhar[mm]īty ucyate | iti | tat* kim idānīṃ hetoḥ sāmarthyam abādha[yai]va sādhyasiddheḥ | sādhyābhāvô hi bādhaka

21b4 pramāṇavṛttiniyata ity abādhāyāṃ sādhyasiddhir iti vyartho he⊙tuḥ | bādhāyām api sādhanasāmarthyābhāvāt* | aniyame na ca bādhakaṃ pramāṇaṃ syāt sādhyābhāvasya ca

21b5 sambhava iti nābādhāyāḥ sāmarthyam* [‖] na ˇ‹ca› bā- below l. 6 +5 dhā'bhāvo 'bādhā |⊙ kin tarhi bādhā[nupa]labdhi[ḥ s]ā puruṣasya kvacid bādhāsambhave pi syād iti sa hetuprayogaviṣayaḥ | kin nu vai he

21b6 tur bbādhopalabdher bbibheti na bādhāyāḥ | yena bādhām anādṛtyānupalabdhau prayoga i[ṣṭ]aḥ | sa tarhi hetuḥ paramārthato bādhāyāḥ bhāva[m] abhāvaṃ vā 'napekṣya bādhānupalabdhau ¦

HB 22a

22a1 prayoktavyaḥ | sa kim arthaṃ prayujyate | sādhyasiddhyartham* | sa kiṃ kvacid bādhāyām api satyāṃ sādhyaṃ sādhayet* yenāsyā nābhāvanirṇṇayaṃ prati yatnaḥ
end of l. 1 kriyate hetuś ca prayujyate | tathā‹pi›

22a2 nābādhitaviṣayatvaṃ hetulakṣaṇaṃ bādhāyām apy asya sāma¦⊙rthyāt* | tathā ca yathānupalambhe bādhāyā bhāvasambhave py abhyupagamya prayogaḥ saṃśayitasyānabhyupagame

22a3 pravṛttyayogāt* | tathā bādhopalabdhāv api prayogo '{mbh?}⊙[bhyu]pagame sati viśeṣābhāvāt* | na bādhāyāṃ samartha iti cet* | yady evaṃ na nirṇṇītabādhā'sambhavaḥ pra¦

22a4 yogam arhati | mā bhūt^{0} prayuktasyāpy asāmarthyam iti | bā⊙dhā'nupalambhe sāmarthyam iti cet* | kim upalambho bādhāṃ vyāpnoti, ye[na] tannivṛttau bādhānivṛttir yato hê

22a5 tor bbādhāsambhavakṛtam asāmarthyan na syāt* | tathāpi vyartho ⊙ het{o}ur bbādhānupalambhād eva sādhyasiddher anupalambhe bādhā'sambhavāt* | upalambhanivṛttāv api bādhā'ni

22a6 vṛttau tadavasthaṃ hetor asāmarthyam ity aprayogaḥ | tasmāt svasādhyabhāvābhāvābhyām anyathāpi bhavan* dharmmiṇi hetur nna kiñcid bhāvayati na vibhāvayatīti na tadupakṣepa□samarthaḥ ||

HB 22b

22b1 tan na bādhā'vinābhāvayoḥ sahabhāva[s] t[e]na nābā-
dhā rūpāntaraṃ | tan nāma tasmād viśeṣaṇāntaram* syāl la-
kṣaṇāntaratvena vopādānam arhati | yadbhāve pi yasyānya-
thābhāvaḥ | tad yathā pakṣa

22b2 dharmmatvaṃ sapakṣe ca bhāva iti | na caitad a-
{vya?va}bādhāyā avinābhāve sati sambhava‡‡tīti | na hetu-
viruddhayoḥ [sādhyav]iparyayāvinābhāvinor viṣaye bādhā
sambhavaḥ | [i]ti na tada

22b3 bhāvaḥ pṛthag anayor llakṣaṇatvena vācyaḥ | tasmān na
hetupra⊙yoge sati pratijñādoṣāṇāṃ sambhavaḥ | [nāpi] ke-
valāyāḥ pratijñāyāḥ prayogo 'stīti na pratijñādoṣā¦

22b4 vācyāḥ || etenaikasaṃkhyāvivakṣāpi pratyuktā | katham
eka⊙ḥ hi svasādhyabhāva eva bhā[v]āt* | tenāvyabhicārī |
tatraiva tadanyo pi tadbādhakasya bhāva eva bhāvād viru-
ddhas te¦

22b5 neti bādha□yā samānaṃ | api ca yo vastuto 'sambhava-
tpratihetuḥ sa kiṃ samyag*jñānaviparyayahetur iṣṭaḥ | ā-
hosvid apradarśitapratihetu‹ḥ› kiṃñ cātaḥ | yady asambha- in l. 5
vatpratihetur a

22b6 lakṣaṇam etad aśakyaniścayatvāt* | hetvabhāvo vā | na
hy aniścitātma[n]aḥ pratipādakadharmmasya tallakṣaṇa-
tvaṃ | saṃdigdhapakṣadharmmatvavat* | nā[p]i [sa]<ṃ>-
digdhalakṣaṇo hetur iti | na kaścid dhetu

HB 23a

23a1 ḥ syāt' | tulyalakṣaṇe hi dṛṣṭaḥ pratiyogisambhavo 'dṛ-
above l. 1 +1 ṣṭapratiyogiṣv a˟‹pi› śaṅkām utpādayati ı viśeṣābhāvāt' | sati
vā viśeṣe sa eva hetulakṣaṇaṃ tato hi hetur e

23a2 kāntena nirastapratipakṣaḥ svasādhyaṃ niścāyayatīti |
atallakṣaṇo na hetuḥ syāt' | tathā caikasaṃkhyāvivakṣā
vyarthā | ato viruddhāvyabhicārilakṣaṇaṃ hīyeta |

23a3 svalakṣaṇayuktayor hetvô□r ekatra virodhenopa⊙nipāte
viruddhâvyabhicārīti | na ca tasya viśeṣasya rūpaṃ nirddi-
śyate | yat pratītya pratiyogi

23a4 sambhavāsambhavāv utpaśyāmaḥ | tasmān nāsty eva ‡
⊙ viśeṣa iti sarvvatra śaṅkayā bhavitavyam* | dṛṣṭaprati-
hetor api hetoḥ prāg itareṇa na kaści

23a5 d viśeṣo lakṣyate | na ca sambhavatpratihetūnām api
sarvvadā tadupalabdhiḥ | atiśayavatī tu prajñotprekṣaṇī dṛ-
ṣṭā tenāniścayaḥ sambhavāsambhavayo

23a6 r ı iti | aniścitalakṣaṇatvān na kaścid dhetuḥ syāt' |
{··········} | athāpradarśita‡pratihetur hetuḥ | yathāha |
yadā tarhi śabdatvaṃ nityam abhyupai

HB 23b

23b1 ti tadāyaṃ hetu‡r eva syāt' | yady atrānityatvahetuṃ kṛtakatvādikam api kaścin na nirddêśayed iti | idam idānīṃ kaṣṭataraṃ vyasanam āpatitam aprakāśyam asaṃvaraṇīyañ ca ka

23b2 thaṃ nirvvoḍhuṃ śakyê□ta | sa tāvad ayaṃ hetur vvastūni svasādhyatattvaprakṛtīni kṛtvā tatpramāṇakān* puruṣān abhyudayaniḥśreyasābhyāṃ saṃyojya punaḥ pratibhāvatā

23b3 puruṣeṇa hetvantaranidarśanotkīlitasādhana⊙sāmarthyas tāni vastūni tāṃś ca puruṣāṃs tadbhāvasampadaḥ pracyāvya bhraṣṭarājya iva rājā tapovanaṃ

23b4 gacchatīti kiṃ atra brūmaḥ | puruṣapratibhākṛte ⊙ ca sādhanatve kiṃ idānīṃ vastutaḥ sādhanam asādhanam vā | sa ca hetuḥ svabhāvatas taddharma

23b5 bhāvī katham anyathā kriyate ˡ vastūnāṃ svabhāvānyathābhāvasya viruddhobhayasvabhāvasya cābhāvāt* | ata‡ddharmmabhāvī ca katham anya‡dāpi sādha

23b6 naṃ kasyacit* | tasmāt* svabhāvataḥ svasādhyāvinābhāvinor vihitalakṣaṇayoḥ kāryasvabhāvayos tallakṣaṇasya pratihetor abhā

HB 24a

24a1 vāt' | ala‡kṣaṇam ekasaṃkhyāvivakṣā vyavacchedyābhāvāt' || jñānaṃ punar aliṅgadharmmaḥ '| kathaṃ liṅgasya lakṣaṇaṃ syāt' | kiṃrūpāl liṅgād arthaḥ pratipattavya iti cintāyāṃ prati

24a2 pattur avisamvādakasya rūpam u□cyate ' yaddarśanād ayaṃ sādhanāsādhane pravivecya tasyeṣṭārthasannidhānapratyayāt* pravarttate | tatra yad asyātmarūpaṃ tal lakṣa-
in l. 2 ṇaṃ na pa‹ra›rūpaṃ

24a3 pratipattijanmany upayogamātrāt* | tallakṣaṇatve ⊙ 'tiprasaṅgāt' | evaṃ hi prameyapuruṣādīnām api tallakṣaṇatvaṃ syāt' | na hi teṣv apy asatsu liṅgi

24a4 ni jñānam iti । niścitagrahaṇaṃ tarhi na karttavyaṃ | na । na ka⊙rttavyaṃ tasyānyārthatvāt' | sapakṣavipakṣayor darśanādarśanābhyāṃ gamakaṃ hetum icchatāṃ naivaṃ samarthaḥ

24a5 rtho ‡‡‡ hetur bhavati ' darśanādarśanayoḥ sator apy agamakatvāt' | tena bhāvābhāvābhyāṃ gamaka iti jñāpanārthaṃ niścitagrahaṇaṃ । tena na pararū

24a6 paṃ lakṣaṇaṃ । liṅgarūpaviśeṣasya tenānabhidhānāt' | tau hi bhāvābhā‡vau tada'bhāvasādhanapramāṇavṛttyā boddhavyau | upāyāntara

HB 24b

24b1 syāsambhavāt' | tena tayoḥ pradarśanāya niścitaśabdaḥ prayukto lakṣaṇe | yady api bhāvābhāvavacanamātreṇāpi tatsādhanapramāṇavṛttir ākṣipya

24b2 te | anyathā tayor eva sattā'prasiddheḥ | jñānasattānibandhanatvāt' jñeyasattāvyavasthāyāḥ | sarvvatra sattāvyavasthaiva pramāṇaṃ tat*sādhanam anvā

24b3 karṣatīti ı parārthatvāc ca śāstrapraṇayanasya | tri⊙rūpaṃ liṅgaṃ vaḥ saṃvādakam arthasyeti | tad rūpaṃ ye na vidanti na teṣāṃ tataḥ pravṛttir iti

24b4 paropalakṣaṇatvād eva jñānaṃ siddham iti | ta⊙thāpi tāv eva bhāvābhāvau kecid darśanādarśanamātreṇa vyavasthāpayantīti tanniṣe

24b5 dhārtho niścitaśabdaḥ ı sator api bhāvābhāvayor anvayavyatirekayoḥ sattāsaṃśayāt' | yataḥ pramāṇād an{e}ayor niścayaḥ | tadadhīnā

24b6 sattāprasiddhir iti jñāpanāya niścitavacanaṃ kṛtam asmābhiḥ | yato pi bhāvābhāvavacanamātreṇa tatsādhanapramāṇākṣepasiddhiḥ

HB 25a

above l. 1 +1 25a1 ///kṣaṇaṃ | tenaiva ˇ‹niścitagrahaṇenaiva› gatatvāt' | upanayārtha‡vat pakṣadharmmatvāt' |ˡˡ anvayavyatirekayor api tarhi na pṛthaktvaṃ | ekapray[o]///

25a2 /// sapakṣavipakṣayo⊙r bhāvābhāvayor aparasparāpekṣatvād ekaṃ vākyam ubhayaṃ gamayatīty ucyate | naiko 'rtho

25a3 ///s tadabhāve 'vaśyam a⊙bhāvaś ca parasparam ākṣipataḥ | vacanam etad ubhayaṃ sāmarthyād ākṣipati | ekasyāpi ni¦

25a4 ///kṣepanāntarīyakatvā⊙t' | na punaḥ kevalau bhāvābhāvau parasparam ākṣipataḥ | niyamavantau ca na kevalau ¦

25a5 ///t' | tasmāt tatraiva bhāva iti na bhāva evocyate | below l. 6 +5 netareṇāpy abhāva eva | yena bhāvo 'bhāvo ‸‹vā› dvitīyam ākṣipe¦

25a6 ///ṇāt trailakṣaṇyād avyatirekād iti na lakṣaṇāntaraṃ | tasmān na hetuḥ ṣaḍlakṣaṇa iti || ~ || hetubindur nnāma prakara

HB 25b

25b1 /// kṛtir ācāryasyāśeṣavidaḥ śrīdharmakīrtteḥ || ~ ||

The Srinagar fragment—edited by Klaus Wille

In the transliteration the following symbols are used: + = lost *akṣara*; () = restored *akṣara*; [] = damaged *akṣara*; {} = superfluous *akṣara*; {{}} = cancelled by correction mark; .. = illegible *akṣara*; . = single element thereof; ..̱/a̱ = covered *akṣara* or part thereof by a fold in the leaf; /// = leaf broken off here; | = *daṇḍa*; * = *virāma*; ' = *avagraha*, not written in the manuscript; ẖ = *jihvāmūlīya*; substitution of *va* for *ba*.

recto

1 /// [s s](a)hitaḥ | svabhāvabhedalakṣaṇatvād bhāvabheda-sya | na hi sa sāhitye 'pi pararūpe[ṇ]. [k]. .. ..

2 /// [rāmaḥ] | yasyāpi kṣaṇiko bhāvas tasya kin na kevalaẖ karoti | karoty eva yadi .. t* k[i]n na

3 /// s[ya] k[ṛ]yā | sa katham ekakṣaṇabhāvy anyathā bhavet* | yaś ca bhavati sa {sa} eva na bhavat[ī](ṯ)[i n]āyaṃ pra

4 /// + + .. taddhetvor virodhāt* | yo 'pi manyate akṣepakri-yādharmaiva sa tasya sva .. ..̱ [n](a) sa .. +

5 /// + + + .. [te]bhya eva jāyate na kevalebhya iti | tasyāpi kathaṃ sa kevala[ẖ ka̱]roty eva k[ā](r)y(aṃ)

6 /// + + + + [ẖ k](a)ro[t]y [e]veti cet* | katham idānīm a-[kṣe]pakriyāsvabhāvaḥ | nanv e[tad] eva paridīpi

verso

1 /// + + + + .. ram apekṣamāṇaṃ katham upekṣeta | param an{{n}}ādya[21]tyenat prasahya kuryāt* | e[v](aṃ) hy (a)ne[n]ā[t]m(a)[n](a)ḥ

2 /// + + + (ḫ) [k](e)[v](a)lād anutpatti[r] uktā bhavati | sa kevalo 'pi samarthasvabhāva iti ta[ta] utpattiḥ | ete

3 /// + + + + .. [l]yavitudyamānamarmā viklavaṃ vikrośatīty upekṣām arhati | ta[smād i]dam e .. + +

4 /// + + + + (bh)ā[v]ā[n]āṃ na saṃbhavan pṛthagbhāvānām akṣaṇikānām* | pṛthakkaraṇasaṃbhavena sa[h]_ .. [ritv](a)m iya

5 /// + + .. + ... yathā [t]aṇḍulabījādibhyaḥ odanāṅkurādijanmani | dahano[dak]_ [pṛ]thivyāda

6 /// [n]tānāśra[yeṇo]{no}cyate na dravyāśrayeṇa | kṣaṇike dravye viśeṣānut[pa]tt[e]ḥ | na [h]i [ta]

---

[21] Scribal error for °*dṛ*°.

Analytic Survey

0. **Introduction** 1,1–5

0.1 Motive and purpose of this work 1,2–3

0.2 Programmatic stanza: definition of the logical reason (*hetu*); three types of the reason; justification of these types; definition of apparent reasons (*hetvābhāsa*) 1,4–5

0.3 Explanation of this stanza 1,6–39,17

1. *pakṣa* (the subject) definition as property bearer (*dharmin*) and purpose of this work 1,6–2,5

1.1 Refutation of Īśvarasena's objection against a synecdochic definition 1,6–2,3

1.2 Refutation of the objection: The reason defined as property of the subject (*pakṣa*) would be uncommon (*asādhāraṇa*). 2,3–5

2. *tadaṃśa*: determination of „part" or „attribute" (*aṃśa*) as property of the subject 2,6

3. *vyāpti* (pervasion): definition and ascertainment of pervasion 2,7–6,12

3.1 The qualification of the reason as „property of the subject" (*pakṣa*) and as „pervaded by a part (= property) of it" imply an indication of common presence (*anvaya*) and common absence (*vyatireka*) as ascertained. 2,8–11

3.2 Ascertainment (*niścaya*) of the reason as property of the subject is the establishment through perception or inference; this is a recollecting cognition (*smārta*). 2,12–3,2

a. **Digression**: On ascertainment (*niścaya*) as valid cognition (*pramāṇa*) 3,3–5,3

a.1 Only the first seeing is a valid cognition. 3,3–5,3

a.2 Why the ascertainment as recollection is not a valid cognition 3,4–5,3

a.21 Denial of an undesired consequence for the phases of perception following the first one 4,11–5,2

(a.2) Résumé: Also other concepts in the inferential process, such as of property, property-bearer, reason and so on, are not valid cognitions. 5,2–3

3.3 Ascertainment of common presence (*anvaya*) 5,4–6,4

3.31 in the case of essence^{C} (*svabhāva*)[22] as reason 5,4–7

3.32 in the case of effect (*kārya*) as reason 5,8–6,2

3.33 in the case of non-perception (*anupalabdhi*) as reason 6,3–4

3.4 Ascertainment of common absence (*vyatireka*) 6,5–12

3.41 in the case of essence^{C} and effect as reason 6,5–10

3.42 in the case of non-perception as reason 6,11–12

4. *tridhaiva saḥ, avinābhāvaniyamāt*: Three types of reason are essence^{C}, effect and non-perception, because the invariable logical nexus (*avinābhāva*) is restricted only to these. 6,13–39,17

[22] The term *svabhāva* in Dharmakīrti's logical and ontological thought has two meanings: "essential property" and "essence, nature" of some entity. In order to keep the ambivalence of this term alive and visible I translate both concepts with the same word "essence". But in order to indicate the differentiation required by the context I add a superscript ^{C} (= concept) to "essence" identifying essence as a concept, and a superscript ^{N} (= nature) identifying essence as nature. Cf. Steinkellner 2013: I. xxxv–xxxvi.

4.1 **Essence^c^ (*svabhāva*) as reason** 7,3–28,3

4.10 Definition: The domain of essence^c^ as reason is a property to be proven that follows the mere presence of the proving property. 7,3

4.11 Explanation of this definition: 7,3–8

4.111 Conceptual difference and real identity 7,3–4

4.112 The purpose of the attribute „that follows the mere presence of the proving property" is the negation of a property caused by other entities as being an essence^c^. 7,4–8

4.12 Two types of formulation of this reason: in terms of similarity (*sādharmyeṇa*) and of dissimilarity (*vaidharmyeṇa*) 7,8–13

4.13 These two are sufficient in a proof. Refutation of other members in a proof 8,1–9,8

4.131 The formulation of a thesis (*pratijñā*) is superfluous. 8,1–9,4

4.132 The formulation of an application (*upanaya*), a conclusion (*nigamana*) and of other members, such as in the ten-membered proof of Vindhyavāsin, are superfluous. 9,5–8

4.14 The sequence of the formulations of pervasion and reason is not compulsive. 9,9–10

4.15 The communication of a pervasion differs only in terms of its formulation (*prayoga*). Thus, only one type of formulation is necessary. 9,11–10,7

4.151 Refutation of a reason for the necessity of formulating common absence in addition to common presence 10,5–7

b. **Digression**: The cognition of pervasion between the essential 10,8–28,3
properties of beingness (*sattva*) and of having a ceasing essence[N] (*naśvarasvabhāvatva*) in the case of the momentariness (*kṣaṇikatva*) of entities

b.1 This cognition is based on the fact that an external cause of 10,9–27,7
cessation is impossible (*vināśahetvayoga*). Entities cease only due to their essence[N].

b.11 Cessation is not due to other causes than their own be- 10,11–11,5
cause such other casues are incapable (*asāmarthyāt*).

b.111 An external cause of cessation does not cause the es- 10,11–12
sence[N] of an entity (*bhāvasvabhāva*).

b.112 It does not cause another entity (*bhāvāntara*). 10,12–11,2

b.113 It does not cause the absence of an entity (*bhāvābhā*- 11,2–5
va).

b.12 Because such other causes would be useless (*vaiya*- 11,6–27,4
rthyāt).

b.121 Dharmakīrti's position: An entity ceases by itself on 11,6–12
account of having a ceasing essence[N].

b.122 Defence of this position: 21,1–25,12

Objection: The reason for the uselesseness of an external cause is inconclusive (*anekānta*) because an entity may be ceasing, yet for its cessation depend on external causes, like a seed that never produces a sprout alone but in dependence on other causes, such as water and so on.

Answer: Only the last specific phase of a seed is the cause of the sprout. There is no temporal unity in an entity.

b.1221 Refutation of objections based on difficulties if several causes (i.e., a complex of causes) are present 12,10–25,5

b.12211 Why the last phases of the different causes do not produce the effect respectively alone 12,10–11

b.12212 Why the other causes (*sahakārin*) are active when one alone is capable 13,1–5

b.12213 Why the different causes do not produce different effects respectively 13,6–8

b.12214 The different causes bring about different properties in the single effect. Example of the single effect of a pot 13,9–16,7

b.122141 Refutation of the position: Since the figure (*saṃsthāna*) of a pot is different from its substance clay, the effects are different. 14,6–15,4

(b.12214) A single effect is produced by plural causes with an essence[N] characterized in specific ways. Example of visual cognition 15,5–16,7

b.12215 Defence of auxiliary function (*sahakriyā*) in momentary causes. Definition of auxiliary function. The last phases of momentary causes come about as being together (*saha*) capable of producing one and the same effect. 16,8–25,5

b.122151 Causes come about as being capable on account of their own causes. 17,6–18,7

b.1221511 Refutation of the position: A cause could be capable also when other causes are absent. 17,7–11

(b.122151) Capable for producing an effect is a complex of 17,12–18,7
causes. A specific cause as ground for the mutual approximation of the different causes in the complex is cause of this capable complex.

b.1221512 Refutation of the position: Something is ca- 18,8–14
pable of producing an effect, but produces together with other causes, not alone.

b.122152 Refutations of theorems on the arising of capa- 19,1–22,3
bility in non-momentary causes

b.1221521 Alternative: A capable entity is different or 19,1–3
not different from an earlier incapable one. If different, something new arises; if not different, nothing arises.

b.1221522 Refutation of the position: A lasting entity is 19,1–3
essentially capable.

b.1221523 Refutation of the position: A lasting entity is 20,6–13
not capable on its own, but in connection with other entities.

b.1221524 Refutation of the position: A lasting entity is 21,1–11
capable but its effect depends on the presence of other causes.

(b.122152) Conclusion: Auxiliary function is only possible 22,1–3
for momentary entities that do not occur separately.

b.122153 Explanation of auxiliary function as bearing on a continuum of phases (*santānopakāra*). Example of the arising of sprout from seed. Determination of auxiliary function as generating a special feature (*viśeṣotpādana*) in regard to the unreal continuum, not in regard to the momentary entity. Difference of auxiliary function in the case of sense cognition 22,4–25,5

b.1221531 Refutation of an objection against the arising of a special feature in momentary entities: Also in the case of a continuum the auxiliary function consists in the production of one and the same effect by plural causes. The arising of special features explained 23,6–25,5

(b.122) Conclusion: Non-momentary causes can have no auxiliary function, neither by way of causing one and the same effect, nor by way of causing a special feature in a continuum of phases. 25,6–12

b.123 Summary of the arguments for the unchangeability of an essence[N] through external causes. Supplement: The melting of copper etc. 25,13–27,4

b.1231 Refutation of the position: An entity is lasting and ceases through another. Cessation is not another essence[N], only a disappearance of the entity (*bhāvapracyuti*). 26,10–27,4

(b.1) Conclusion of the establishment of the impossibility of an external cause for the cessation of entities 27,5–7

(b.) Summary on the pervasion between the properties of beingness (*sattva*) and of having a ceasing essence[N] (*naśvarasvabhāvatva*) 27,8–10 b.2 Refutation of an objection against the general validity of this pervasion by means of proving this pervasion in terms of the logical structure of the proof from beingness (*sattvā-numāna*) 27,11–28,3

4.2 **Effect (*kārya*) as reason** 28,4–30,11

4.20 The domain of effect as reason is a different entity as property to be proven (*sādhya*). 28,4

4.21 Refutation of the unacceptable consequence that the relationship between inferring and inferred would hold for all properties since the relation between producing and produced is given throughout. The relationship is restricted to certain properties of cause and effect. 28,5–11

4.22 The pervasion between an effect and a cause is established through the establishment of the relation between cause and effect. 28,12–30,1

4.221 Explanation of cases seemingly arising from something different in kind (*vijātīya*), such as water lilies from cow dung 29,10–30,1

4.3 **Non-perception (*anupalabdhi*) as reason** 31,1–39,15

4.30 The domain of non-perception of a perceptible is the absence of something or the treatment of something as absent (*abhāvavyavahāra*) 31,1–2

c. **Digression:** The nature of non-perception 31,3–39,3

c.1 Dharmakīrti's position: 31,3–32,2

c.11 Definition of non-perception 31,3–32,2

c.111 As property of the perceiver non-perception is with im- 31,3–5
plicative negation (*paryudāsa*) a perception other than
the perception of the absent entity.

c.112 As property of the perceived non-perception is the fac- 31,5–7
ulty of an entity for perception other than the absent
entity.

c.113 Determination of otherness (*anyatva*) in this context 31,8–32,2

c.2 Defence of this position: 32,3–39,3

c.21 Non-perception is absence as presence of something 32,3–7
other or of another perception with implicative negation
(*paryudāsa*), not with simple negation (*pratiṣedhamātra*).

c.22 The presence of something other or of another percep- 32,8–38,17
tion do not prove the absence of something, but are the
same.

c.221 The presence of something other does not prove the 33,1–38,6
absence of an entity,

c.2211 because the absence of something is not known as 33,2–4
being different from the presence of the other,

c.2212 and because there is no logical relationship between 33,5–38,6
the presence of the other and the absence of an enti-
ty.

c.22121 There is no relationship between object and sub- 33,9–34,15
ject (*viṣayaviṣayibhāva*) like that between word
meaning.

c.221211 When proving the absence of something 34,1–15
through the presence of another, the property to
be proven (*sādhya*) would not be a composite
of property and property-bearer. The absent entity and the location cannot be composite since
the location is the other.

c.2212111 The relationship cannot be one on the basis of the general and the particular (*sāmānyaviśeṣabhāva*). 34, 9–15

c.22122 Opposition (*virodha*) is not a relationship. 35, 1–6

c.22123 The cognition of the absence of something through the cognition of the presence of something else is possible without a relationship. 35, 7–38, 6

c.221231 Absence is not cognized through non-cognition (*anupalambha*). Refutation of Kumārila's theory 36, 1–7

c.221232 Absence of something other is not cognized through perception of an entity. 36, 8–12

c.221233 Defence of the theorem that the determination of one entity excludes only that other entity which, if present, would be perceived. There is no third possibility beyond being the one or the other. 36, 13–38,

c.222 The other perception does not prove the absence of an entity because there is no relationship, 38, 7–17

c.2221 since the absence of an entity is the case only together with the other perception. 38, 9–17

c.23 Conclusion of the defence: Absence of something is never proved through a logical mark (*liṅga*), since the presence of something else is already established by non-perception defined as perception of something other. It can, however, serve to prove the treatment in regard to something's absence when someone is not aware of the appropriate treatment. 39, 1–3

4.31 The three basic types of non-perception: of a cause (*kāraṇānupalabdhi*), of a pervading property (*vyāpakānupalabdhi*), of an essence[N] (*svabhāvānupalabdhi*) 39,4–15

4.311 The first two non-perceptions cannot be used as reasons in regard to invisibles (*parokṣa*). 39,10–15

(4.) Conclusion of the explanation of the three types of reason 39,16–17

d. **Supplement:** Critique of Īśvarasena's theorem of six characteristics of a logical reason (*ṣaḍlakṣaṇo hetu*) 40,1–47,7

d.1 Refutation of the fourth, that its object, the property to be proven (*sādhya*), has not been invalidated by perception or inference (*abādhitaviṣayatva*) 40,3–42,13

d.11 There is a contradiction (*virodha*) between invalidation and an invariable relationship. 40,3–41,4

d.111 Refutation of the proposal to avoid the contradiction by reference to different property-bearers 40,9–41,4

d.112 Refutation of the proposal to avoid uselessness of the reason when no invalidation is present by explaining non-invalidation as non-cognition of invalidation 41,5–42,6

d.1121 Refutation of the position: The reason is incapable when invalidation occurs. 41,6–17

d.1122 Refutation of the position: The reason is capable when invalidation is not cognized. 41,18–42,6

d.12 Invalidation of the reason is impossible without an invariable relationship. Therefore the faults of a thesis (*pratijñādoṣa*) are also impossible. 42,7–13

d.2 Refutation of the fifth, that a singular of the reason is meant (*ekasāṅkhyāvivakṣā*) 42,14–44,15

d.21 This characteristic is refuted through the refutation of the fourth characteristic. 42,14–16

d.22 Specific refutation with an alternative: 43,1–44,1

d.221 Refutation of the first alternative: If there is no counter-reason, the reason is correct. 43,3–17

d.222 Refutation of the second alternative: If a counter-reason is not indicated, the reason is correct. 44,1–12

d.2221 Rectification of a misplaced appeal to a statement by Dignāga 44,1–8

d.2222 The correctness of a reason does not depend on the imagination of counter-reasons. 44,9–12

d.23 Conclusion: There is no counter-reason in the case of essence[C] or effect as reasons. Thus, this characteristic is none. 44,13–15

d.3 Refutation of the sixth, that the reason is known (*jñātatva*) 44,16–47,6

d.31 Cognition (*jñāna*) does not satisfy the conditions of a reason's characteristic. 44,16–46,

d.311 Refutation of an objection against the use of the term "ascertained" (*niścita*) in the definition of a reason 45,6–46,5

d.3111 The purpose of the term "ascertained" and the purpose of the specific mention of this term 45,7–46,5

d.32 The cognition is already implied by the second and third characteristics. 46,6–47,6

d.321 Refutation of the consequence that common presence and common absence would also not be separate characteristics 46,9–47,6

(d.) Conclusion 47,7

(0.3) Colophon 47,8–9

Bibliography

General Abbreviations

AASP	Austrian Academy of Sciences Press
ATBS	Arbeitskreis für Tibetische Buddhistische Studien Universität Wien
BBS	Bauddha Bharati Series
BKGA	Beiträge zur Kultur- und Geistesgeschichte Asiens
ChSS	Chowkhambā Sanskrit Series
CTPH	China Tibetology Publishing House
CTRC	China Tibetology Research Center
D	Derge Edition, Tokyo
Ed./ed.	Edition, edited
em.	emended
n.	note(s)
GOS	Gaekwad's Oriental Series
IsMEO	Istituto Italiano per il Medio ed Estremo Oriente
JBORS	*Journal of Bihar and Orissa Research Society*
JMJG	Jñānapīṭha Mūrtidevī Jaina Granthamālā
KPJRI	Kashi Prasad Jayaswal Research Institute
KSTSt	Kashmir Series of Texts and Studies
LDS	Lālbhāī Dalpatbhāī Series

P	Peking Edition, Tokyo
s.	see
SOR	Serie Orientale Roma
SOS	Saraswati Oriental Series
STTAR	Sanskrit Texts from the Tibetan Autonomous Region
T	Tibetan translation as edited in HB_{St}
TSWS	Tibetan Sanskrit Works Series
VKSKSO	Veröffentlichungen der Kommission für Sprachen und Kulturen Süd- und Ostasiens
VÖAW	Verlag der Österreichischen Akademie der Wissenschaften
WSTB	Wiener Studien zur Tibetologie und Buddhismuskunde
WZKS	*Wiener Zeitschrift für die Kunde Südasiens*

Primary Literature

AAĀ — Abhisamayālaṅkārāloka (Haribhadra) – *Abhisamayālaṃkārālokā Prajñāpāramitāvyākhyā (commentary on Aṣṭasāhasrikā-Prajñāpāramitā) by Haribhadra together with the text commented on*. Ed. Unrai Wogihara. Parts I and II. Tokyo: The Toyo Bunko 1932–1935

AJP — Anekāntajayapatākā (Haribhadra Sūri) – *Anekāntajayapatākā by Haribhadra Sūri. With his own commentary and Municandra Sūri's supercommentary*. 2 Vols. Critically edited with an introduction by H. R. Kāpadīā. (GOS 88, 105) Baroda: Oriental Institute 1940, 1947

AR — Anupalabdhirahasya (Jñānaśrīmitra) – Birgit Kellner, *Jñānaśrīmitra's Anupalabdhirahasya and Sarvaśabdābhāvacarcā. A Critical Edition with a Survey of his Anupalabdhi-Theory*. (WSTB 67) Wien: ATBS 2007

AS — Aṣṭasahasrī (Vidyānanda) – *Aṣṭasahasrī sakalatārkikacakracūḍāmaṇi-syādvādavidyāpatinā Śrī-Vidyānandasvāminā nirmitā ...*. Ed. Vaṃśīdhara. Mumbāpurī: Nirṇaya Sāgara Press 1915

ĪPVV — Īśvarapratyabhijñāvivṛtivimarśiṇī (Abhinavagupta) – *The Īśvarapratyabhijñā Vivritivimarśinī by Abhinavagupta*. 3 vols. Ed. Madhusūdan Kaul Shāstrī. (KSTSt 60, 62, 65) Srinagar: Research Department, Jammu and Kashmir Government 1938–1943. [Reprint: Delhi, Akay Book Corporation 1987]

Utp — Utpādādisiddhiḥ (Candrasenasūri) – *Anavādyānupamavedacatuṣṭayavidhānavedhaḥ śrī Hemacandragurubhrātṛ-śrī-Pradyumnasūricaraṇa-caṃcarika śrī-Candrasenasūrisūtritā svopajñā śrī-Utpādādisiddhiḥ.* Prakāśayitrī ... śvetāṃbarasaṃsthā. Gopīpurā 1936

J — Jñānaśrīmitranibandhāvali (Jñānaśrīmitra) – *Jñānaśrīmitranibandhāvali (Buddhist Philosophical Works of Jñānaśrīmitra).* Ed. Anantalal Thakur. (TSWS 5) Patna: KPJRI 1987

TBV — Tattvabodhavidhāyinī (Abhayadevasūri) – *Saṃmatitarkaprakaraṇa by Siddhasena Divākara with Abhayadevasūri's Commentary Tattvabodhavidhāyinī.* 5 vols. Ed. S. Sanghavi and B. Doshi. Ahmedabad 1921–1931

TBh — Tarkabhāṣā (Mokṣākaragupta) – *Tarkabhasha and Vadasthana of Mokshakaragupta and Jitaripada.* Ed. H. R. Rangaswami Iyengar. Mysore 1952

TR — Tarkarahasya – Hideomi Yaita, *Bukkyō Chishikiron no ganten kenkyū – Yogaron inmyō, Dharmottaraṭippanaka, Tarkarahasya* [Three Sanskrit Texts from the Buddhist *Pramāṇa*-Tradition – The *Hetuvidyā* Section in the *Yogācārabhūmi*, the *Dharmottaraṭippanaka*, and the *Tarkarahasya*]. (Monograph Series 4) Narita: Naritasan Shinshōji 2005, 261–407 (= 1*–72*)

TSP — Tattvasaṅgrahapañjikā (Kamalaśīla) – *The Tattvasaṅgraha of Ācārya Shāntarakṣita with the commentary 'Pañjikā' of Shrī Kamalshīla.* Ed. Swami Dwarikadas Shastri. 2 vols, (BBS 1,2) Varanasi 1968

DAṬ Dravyālaṅkāraṭīkā (Rāmacandra and Guṇacandra) – *Ācārya Ramacandra and Gunacandra's Dravyālaṅkāra. With Auto-Commentary.* Ed. Muni Shri Jambuvijayaji. (LDS 126) Ahmedabad 2001

DhPr Dharmottarapradīpa (Durvekamiśra) – *Paṇḍita Durveka Miśra's Dharmottarapradīpa [Being a sub-commentary on Dharmottara's Nyāyabinduṭīkā, a commentary on Dharmakīrti's Nyāyabindu].* Ed. Dalsukhbhai Malvania. (TSWS 2) Patna: KPJRI 1955

NKaṇḍ Nyāyakaṇḍalī (Śrīdhara) – *Nyāyakandalī being a commentary on Praśastapādabhāṣya, with three sub-commentaries.* Ed. J. S. Jetly and Vasant G. Parikh. (GOS 174) Vadodara: Oriental Institute 1991

NBhū Nyāyabhūṣaṇam (Bhāsarvajña) – *Śrīmadācārya-Bhāsarvajña-praṇītasya Nyāyasārasya svopajñaṃ vyākhyānaṃ Nyāyabhūṣaṇam.* Ed. Svāmī Yogīndrānanda. (Ṣaḍdarśanaprakāśanagranthamālā 1) Vārāṇasī: Ṣaḍdarśanaprakāśanapratiṣṭhānam 1968

NBṬ *Nyāyabinduṭīkā* (Dharmottara) – cf. DhPr

NM I, II Nyāyamañjarī (Jayanta) – *Nyāyamañjarī of Jayantabhaṭṭa with Ṭippaṇī – Nyāyasaurabha by the Editor.* 2 vols. Critically ed. K. S. Varadācārya. (University of Mysore, Oriental Research Institute Series 116, 139) Mysore: Oriental Research Institute 1969, 1983

NMak *Nyayamakaranda. A Treatise on Vedanta Philosophy by Śree Ānanda Bodha Bhaṭṭārakāchārya with a commentary by Chitsukh Muni, Pramānamālā and Nyāyadīpāvalī.* Ed. Swāmi Bālarāma Udaseen Māndālika. (ChSS 38, 62, 87, 117) Benares 1907

NVTṬ Nyāyavārttikatātparyaṭīkā (Vācaspatimiśra) – *Nyāyavārttikatātparyaṭīkā of Vācaspatimiśra.* Ed. Anantalal Thakur. New Delhi: Indian Council of Philosophical Research 1996

NVinV Nyāyaviniścayavivaraṇa (Vādirāja Sūri) – *Nyāya Viniścaya Vivaraṇa of Śrī Vādirāja Sūri, the commentary on Bhaṭṭākalankadeva's Nyāya Viniścaya.* 2 vols. Ed. Mahendra Kumār Jain. (JMJG, Sanskrit Grantha 3, 12) Banaras: Bhāratīya Jñānapīṭha, Kashi 1949, 1954

PPar II Laghuprāmāṇyaparīkṣā (Dharmottara) – Helmut Krasser, *Dharmottaras kurze Untersuchung der Gültigkeit einer Erkenntnis. Laghuprāmāṇyaparīkṣā. Teil 1: Tibetischer Text und Sanskritmaterialien.* (BKGA 7) Wien: VÖAW 1991

PMim Pramāṇamīmāṃsā (Hemacandra) – *Pramāṇa Mīmāṃsā of Kalikāla sarvajña Śrī Hemacandrācārya.* Ed. Sukhalāljī Saṅghavī, Mahendra Kumar, Dalsukh Mālvaṇīā. (SOS 1) Ahmedabad: Saraswati Pustak Bhandar 1989

PV 1 Pramāṇavārttika (Dharmakīrti), chapter 1 (*svārthānumāna*)[23] – cf. PVSV

PV 2,3,4 Pramāṇavārttika (Dharmakīrti), chapters 2, 3, 4 – *Dharmakīrti's Pramāṇavārttika with a commentary by Manorathanandin.* Ed. Rāhula Sāṅkṛtyāyana. (Appendix to *JBORS* 24–26) Patna 1938–1940

[23] Since 2013 I do not continue my previous habit of counting the stanzas of PV 1 differently from Gnoli's edition by adding 2.

PVA Pramāṇavārttikālaṅkāra (Prajñākaragupta) – *Pramāṇavārtikabhāshyam or Vārtikālaṅkāraḥ of Prajñākaragupta (Being a commentary on Dharmakīrti's Pramāṇavārtikam).* Ed. Rāhula Sāṅkṛtyāyana. (TSWS 1) Patna: KPJRI 1953

PVin 1 Pramāṇaviniścaya (Dharmakīrti), Chapter 1 – *Dharmakīrti's Pramāṇaviniścaya. Chapters 1 and 2.* Critically ed. Ernst Steinkellner. (STTAR 2) Beijing–Vienna: CTPH–AASP 2007

PVin 2 Pramāṇaviniścaya (Dharmakīrti), Chapter 2 – see PVin 1

PVin 3 Pramāṇaviniścaya (Dharmakīrti), Chapter 3 – *Dharmakīrti's Pramāṇaviniścaya. Chapter 3.* Critically edited by Pascale Hugon and Toru Tomabechi. (STTAR 8) Beijing–Vienna: CTPH– AASP 2011

PVinṬ(a) Pramāṇaviniścayaṭīkā (Dharmottara) – Ernst Steinkellner und Helmut Krasser, *Dharmottaras Exkurs zur Definition gültiger Erkenntnis im Pramāṇaviniścaya. Tibetischer Text, Sanskritmaterialien und Übersetzung.* (BKGA 2) Wien: VÖAW 1989

PVṬ$_{t}$ Pramāṇavārttikaṭīkā (Śākyabuddhi), Chapter 1 – P 5718, Je 1b-348a8, Ñe 1b–85b2; D 4420, Je 1b–Ne 282a7

PVV Pramāṇavārttikavṛtti (Manorathanandin) – *Dharmakīrti's Pramāṇavārttika with a commentary by Manorathanandin.* Ed. Rāhula Sāṅkṛtyāyana. (Appendix to *JBORS* 24–26) Patna 1938–1940

PVSV — Pramāṇavārttika(sva)vṛtti (Dharmakīrti) – Raniero Gnoli, *The Pramāṇavārttikam of Dharmakīrti. The First Chapter with the Autocommentary.* (SOR 23) Roma: IsMEO 1960

PSṬ 2 — Pramāṇasamuccayaṭīkā (Jinendrabuddhi) chapter 2 – *Jinendrabuddhi's Viśālāmalavatī Pramāṇasamuccayaṭīkā Chapter 2. Part I.* Ed. Horst Lasic, Helmut Krasser, Ernst Steinkellner. (STTAR 15/1) Beijing–Vienna: CTPH–AASP 2012

PSṬ 3 — Pramāṇasamuccayaṭīkā (Jinendrabuddhi) chapter 3 – Photostat copy of the Norbulingka manuscript in the library of the CTRC (box 44, ff. 99b7–169b3)

PS(V) — Pramāṇasamuccaya(vṛtti) (Dignāga) – translated by Vasudhararakṣita and Seṅ rgyal: P 5701, Ce 13a6–93b4; translated by Kanakavarman and Dad pa'i śes rab: P 5702, Ce 93b4–177a7

BCAP — Bodhicaryāvatārapañjikā (Prajñākaramati) – *Bodhicaryāvatāra of Śāntideva with the Commentary Pañjikā of Prajñākaramati.* Ed. P. L. Vaidya. (Buddhist Sanskrit Texts 12) Darbhanga: The Mithila Institute 1960

ms — the Potala manuscript of the *Hetubindu*

msS — the *Hetubindu*-fragment in the Sri Pratap Singh Museum, Srinagar

R — Ratnakīrtinibandhāvali (Ratnakīrti) – *Ratnakīrti-Nibandhāvaliḥ (Buddhist Nyāya Works of Ratnakīrti).* Ed. Anantalal Thakur. (TSWS 3) Patna: KPJRI [2]1975

VNṬ — Vādanyāyaṭīkā (Śāntarakṣita) – *Dharmakīrti's Vādanyāya. With the Commentary of Śāntarakṣita.* Ed. Rāhula Sāṅkṛtyāyana. (Appendix to *JBORS* 21 and 22) Patna 1935–1936

VR Vādarahasya (anonymous) (= Udayananirākaraṇa)[24] – *Ācārya-Ratnakīrti-viracitam Udayananirākaraṇam*. Ed. Raghunath Pandey. (Bibliotheca Indo-Buddhica 10) Delhi: Sri Satguru Publications 1984

Vyom Vyomavatī (Vyomaśivācārya) – *Vyomavatī of Vyomaśivācārya*. Ed. Gaurinath Sastri. Vols. I, II (M. M. Śivakumāraśāstri-Granthamālā 6) Varanasi: Sampurnanand Sanskrit Vishvavidyalaya 1983–1984

SAC Sarvaśabdābhāvacarcā (Jñānaśrīmitra) – see AR

SAS Sarvārthasiddhi (Vedāntadeśika) – *Tattvamuktakalāpaḥ Sarvārthasiddhisametaḥ*. Ed. Aṇṇaṃgarācāryaḥ. (Śrīmad-Vedāntadeśikagrathamālā) Madras: Liberty Press 1941

HB Hetubindu (Dharmakīrti) – the present text

HB_{St} Ernst Steinkellner, *Dharmakīrti's Hetubinduḥ. Teil I. Tibetischer Text und rekonstruierter Sanskrit-Text*. (VKSKSO 4) Graz-Wien-Köln: Hermann Böhlaus Nachf. 1967

HB_t Hetubindu, Tibetan translation ed. in HB_{St}

HBṬ Hetubinduṭīkā (Arcaṭa) – *Hetubinduṭīkā of Bhaṭṭa Arcaṭa with the sub-commentary entitled Āloka of Durveka Miśra*. Ed. Sukhlalji Sanghavi and Muni Shri Jinavijayaji. (GOS 113) Baroda: Oriental Institute 1949

HBṬī$_t$ Hetubinduṭīkā (Vinītadeva) – P 5733, We 123b8–223b6

HBṬĀ Hetubinduṭīkāloka (Durvekamiśra) – see HBṬ

HMu Hetumukha (Dignāga)

[24] For the correct title of this text cf. Bühnemann 1984: 187–188 and Much 1987.

Secondary Literature

Bühnemann 1984 Gudrun Bühnemann, Review of: *Tarkarahasya.* Ed. by Acharya Paramananda Shastri, Patna 1979. *WZKS* 27 (1984), 185–190

Frauwallner 1954 Erich Frauwallner, Die Reihenfolge und Entstehung der Werke Dharmakīrti's. *Asiatica. Festschrift Friedrich Weller*, Leipzig 1954, 142–154 (*Kleine Schriften*, pp. 677–689)

Gokhale 1997 Pradeep P. Gokhale, *Hetubindu of Dharmakīrti. (A Point on Probans). A Sanskrit Version translated with Introduction and Notes.* (Bibliotheca Indo-Buddhica Series 183) Delhi: Sri Satguru Publications 1997

Isaacson 2009 Harunaga Isaacson, Of Critical Editions and Manuscript Reproductions: Remarks apropos of a Critical Edition of *Pramāṇaviniścaya* Chapters 1 and 2. *Manuscript Cultures Newsletter* 2 (2009), 13–20

Jambūvijaya 1981 Muni Jambūvijaya, Jainācāryaśrī-Hemacandrasūrimukhya-śiṣyābhyām ācārya-Rāmacandra-Guṇacandrābhyāṃ viracitāyāṃ Dravyālaṅkāra-svopajñaṭīkāyāṃ Bauddhagranthebhya uddhṛtāḥ pāṭhāḥ. In: Klaus Bruhn und Albrecht Wezler (eds), *Studien zum Jainismus und Buddhismus. Gedenkschrift für Ludwig Alsdorf.* Wiesbaden: Franz Steiner Verlag GmbH 1981, 129–149

Krasser 2014 Helmut Krasser, Indic Buddhist Manuscripts in Vienna: A Sino-Austrian Co-operative Project, with Methodological Remarks on Śāstric "Urtexts". In: Paul Harrison and Jens–Uwe Hartmann (eds), *From Birch Bark to Digital Data: Recent Advances in Buddhist Manuscript Research.*

Papers Presented at the Conference Indic Buddhist Manuscripts: The State of the Field. Stanford, June 15–19 2009. (BKGA 80) Wien: VÖAW 2014, 301–313

Kuijp 2013 Leonard van der Kuijp, Introduction in: Leonard W.J. van der Kuijp and Arthur P. McKeown, *Bcom ldan ral gri (1227–1305) on Indian Buddhist Logic and Epistemology: His Commentary on Dignāga's Pramāṇasamuccaya.* (WSTB 80) Wien: ATBS 2013, xi–cv

Lasic 2011 Horst Lasic, Meditations on the Retrieval of Lost Texts with Special Reference to the Sāṅkhya Section of *Pramāṇasamuccaya*, Chapter 2. *Indogaku Tibettogaku Kenkyū* 15 (2011), 231–243

Luo Zhao 1985 *Budalagong xincang beiye jing mulu* [A catalogue of manuscript preserved at the Potala palace]. Vol. of Tanjur holdings. Unpublished manuscript, July 1985

Moriyama 1991 Seitetsu Moriyama, The Later Mādhyamika and Dharmakīrti. In: Ernst Steinkellner (ed.), *Studies in the Buddhist Epistemological Tradition. Proceedings of the Second International Dharmakīrti Conference, Vienna, June 11–16, 1989*. (BKGA 8) Wien: VÖAW 1991, 199–210

Much 1987 M. T. Much, Review of: *Ācāryaratnakīrtiviracitam Udayananirākaraṇam.* Deciphered and critically edited by Raghunath Pandey. Sri Satguru Publications, Delhi 1984 (Bibliotheca Indo-Buddhica 10). *Buddhist Studies Review* 4.1 (1987), 88–90

Oetke 1993 Claus Oetke, *Bemerkungen zur buddhistischen Doktrin der Momentanheit des Seienden. Dharmakīrtis Sattvānumāna.* (WSTB 29) Wien: ATBS 1993

Ono/Oda/Takashima 1996 Motoi Ono / Jun'ichi Oda / Jun Takashima, KWIC Index to the Sanskrit Texts of Dharmakīrti. *Lexicological Studies* 8 (1996), 1–1150 (www.ikga.oeaw.ac.at/Mat/kwic_dharmakirti.pdf)

Pecchia 2015 Cristina Pecchia, with the assistance of Philip Pierce, *Dharmakīrti on the cessation of suffering. A critical edition with translation and comments of Manorathanandin's Vṛtti and Vibhūticandra's glosses on* Pramāṇavārttika *II.190–216.* (Brill's Indological Library 47) Leiden: Brill 2015

Sandhak n.d. Sandhak [gSaṅ bdag], *Zhongguo zangxue yanjiu zhongxin shouzangde fanwen beiye jing (suowei jiaojuan) mulu* [Catalogue of the Sanskrit manuscripts (microfilms) preserved at the China Tibetology Research Center]. Unpublished manuscript, no date, no place

Steinkellner 1967 Ernst Steinkellner, *Dharmakīrti's Hetubinduḥ. Teil II. Übersetzung und Anmerkungen.* (VKSKSO 5) Graz–Wien–Köln: Hermann Böhlaus Nachf. 1967

Steinkellner 1988 Ernst Steinkellner, Methodological Remarks on the Constitution of Sanskrit Texts from the Buddhist *pramāṇa*-Tradition. *WZKS* 32 (1988), 103–129

Steinkellner 2013 Ernst Steinkellner, *Dharmakīrtis frühe Logik. Annotierte Übersetzung der logischen Teile von* Pramāṇavārttika *1 mit der* Vṛtti. 2 Vols. (Studia Philologica Buddhica, Monograph Series xxix) Tokyo: The International Institute for Buddhist Studies 2013

Steinkellner 2014 Ernst Steinkellner, *The Edition of Śāntarakṣita's Vādanyāyaṭīkā Collated with the Kundeling Manuscript.* (WSTB 82) Wien: ATBS 2014

Steinkellner / Much 1995 Ernst Steinkellner und Michael Torsten Much, *Systematische Übersicht über die buddhistische Sanskrit-Literatur.* (Abhandlungen der Akademie der Wissenschaften in Göttingen, phil.-hist. Klasse 2.214) Göttingen: Vandenhoeck & Ruprecht 1995

Yoshimizu 2003 Chizuko Yoshimizu, Augenblichklichkeit (*kṣaṇikatva*) und Eigenwesen (*svabhāva*). Dharmakīrtis Polemik im Hetubindu. *WZKS* 47 (2003), 197–216

图书在版编目（CIP）数据

法称《因滴论》 ：梵文、英文/(印) 法称著；（奥）斯坦因凯勒等 编校. -- 北京 ：中国藏学出版社，2016.3

ISBN 978-7-80253-879-5

Ⅰ. ①法… Ⅱ. ①法… ②斯...Ⅲ. ①因明（印度逻辑）－梵语、英文 Ⅳ. ①B81-093.51

中国版本图书馆CIP数据核字(2016)第046754号

法称《因滴论》 （奥）斯坦因凯勒等编校

出版：中国藏学出版社

发行：中国藏学出版社

责任编辑：南加才让

封面设计：李建雄

印刷：北京隆昌伟业印刷有限公司

开本：787×1092 1/16

印张：10.25

印次：2016年3月第1版第1次

印数：700

书号：ISBN 978-7-80253-879-5/B · 228

定价：18.50元